we grew with Barbara

by Lotte E. Moise

DILLON PRESS, INC. MINNEAPOLIS, MINNESOTA 55415

©1980 by Dillon Press, Inc. All rights reserved

Dillon Press, Inc., 500 South Third Street
Minneapolis, Minnesota 55415

Printed in the United States of America

Library of Congress Cataloging in Publication Data

Moise, Lotte E.
   As up we grew with Barbara.

   1. Moise, Barbara, 1953- 2. Mentally handicapped
   children—United States—Biography.
   3. Mentally handicapped children—Family
   relationships. 4. Mentally handicapped children—
   Education—United States.   I. Title.
HV894.M64   362.3'092'6   79-25649
ISBN 0-87518-194-5

Contents

Foreword

TWENTY-FIVE YEARS AGO, about the time Barbara Moise was born, the National Association for Retarded Children, as it was then known, published a pamphlet entitled "The Child Nobody Knows." Barbara and her parents indeed faced an uncertain future, a universal ignorance about the particular nature of Barbara's "affliction," an unsympathetic community, and a world that held out little hope for Barbara.

Today, a quarter of a century later, a vastly different situation exists. There is an ever-increasing fund of knowledge, there is growing community acceptance, more and more help is available, and there is hope. This improvement, this truly revolutionary change, is due largely to Lotte and Al Moise and hundreds of parents like them who not only steadily found innovative and imaginative answers to the needs of their own children but who also went forth to leadership positions in the parent movement, spreading the good word and pushing action programs so that other families' children could benefit.

Unprecedented progress has been made, victories

have been won in Congress, in the state house, and in the schoolhouse, with increasing support from allies in the professions, but much still remains to be done.

As up We Grew with Barbara is not just a penetrating, honest, warm and lucid account of this quarter century of progress seen through the eyes of one family, but it will also serve as a call to action, as a guide on how to face the battles still to be won. To be sure, even children with severe and multiple handicaps are today assured an education; to be sure, they have a better chance to get needed medical care and habilitation therapies and increasingly, to reside in the community. But what about their right to be meaningfully occupied, to have access to the labor market, to be good neighbors, and to share in community life as citizens?

There is much to be learned from the steadfastness, the positive outlook, the direct approach which characterize this autobiographical story. Most importantly, Barbara—"the child nobody knew"—emerges from these pages as a real person, a vital member of the family group, even though she now lives away from home, as do her brother and sister. That she is able to do so in spite of the obstacles the family encountered year after year in getting adequate programming for her provides the true inspiration of this book.

And that this could happen, we venture to say, is due in large measure to Lotte Moise's growing capacity to listen to what her daughter was saying, with and without words, during all of Barbara's growing up years. But it was also due to the fact that Al and David and Karen were listening too, that throughout all the many times of crisis Lotte and Al kept their sense of humor, were true to their own values, and stood firm, unintimidated by opposition from bureaucrats or professional experts. Their message brings encouragement and a new sense of direction.

ROSEMARY DYBWAD, *Senior Research Associate*

GUNNAR DYBWAD, *Professor Emeritus, Human Development*

Florence Heller Graduate School for Advanced Studies in Social Welfare Brandeis University

Introduction

BARBARA—OUR THIRD CHILD—developed more slowly than the others. Her presence caused us puzzlement and pain, wondering and warmth, laughter and love—all this with a diagnosis and label of "mental retardation."

Now that she is an adult, we find that she has given us focus, insight, and a more balanced sense of values. "As up we grew with Barbara," I found myself writing about her more and more often. I wanted to tell others in the world out there about our discoveries and new perceptions. Parents can and should be the first line of defense for other parents. We can be the dreamers of dreams of ideally appropriate programs for our sons and daughters, and at the same time their severest critics.

Since this has turned out to be a very personal book, and in order not to embarrass my family, I asked each of them for permission to describe and quote them. Barbara, too. My question to her was, "Is it all right for me to write a book about you? Including a lot of personal happenings?" She said, "It's okay to write about me. Write it down. The part about me Chas [her group home manager] can read too. He does good things for me."

Then I asked her how she thought a book like this could help parents.

"Parents?" she asked. "It might stop them from pushing us around. We want to do things by ourselves!"

So here is Barbara's book. It is offered in the hope that other families who have children with developmental special needs may read it and take heart.

1 *Home Is A Moving Out*

ALL THREE OF OUR CHILDREN are grown up now and live away from home. They return at odd intervals for short weekends or holiday vacations, and they roll in in different ways. Karen zips in and out in her little bright orange car quite often since she lives only one county away. For David it's a bigger planning effort to organize his life and pack his dark red van for a journey from Los Angeles to northern California. Barbara travels on the bus, which arrives in town at eight in the evening. My husband Al and I usually drive to the bus stop to meet her.

There is always that small moment of worry—"did she make the bus?"—until we see her smile and wave through the dark, tinted window. Then the driver gives her a hand down the tall steps and I stretch up to hug her.

Barbara is taller than I. Also larger around. She wears her dark blonde hair in a shaggy cut, which is becoming to her pert, round face. She has blue eyes and an almost snub nose. She is twenty-six, and when she gives her age, people look surprised, as though they think she is younger. She does seem younger, partly because she speaks in abbreviated sentences. Partly because she zeros in on the core of situations and the essence of people's feelings with the directness of a child.

Like the Christmas a few years ago when Barbara was home on vacation, excitedly getting ready for houseguests, festivities, and surprises. We were both puttering around the kitchen when there was a knock on the front door. I opened it and there stood Julie, the youngest daughter of old friends, who have divorced and reorganized their lives elsewhere. Julie is younger than Barbara and has been one of her staunch supporters since they were little girls. Once, when our children were playing together, we mothers noticed Julie take Barbara by the hand and lead her outside. "Where are you two going?" I asked. "Out," said Julie. "I'm going to teach her out of this retarded business."

On that winter day years later, Julie looked far from confident. Stooped, bedraggled in a dirty peacoat, stringy-haired, she looked defeated. I heard that she had been messing around with dope, experimenting with men, and trying in a disorganized fashion to find her own way. I had tried to let her know through her mother that she was welcome to come to our house anytime if she wanted to talk. Now I was glad she had come. Barbara knew nothing of her troubles. She turned around, recognized her old friend, and shouted "Julie Ray!"— and then slowly—"Why are you so sad?" Julie put her head on my shoulder and cried.

It happened again the last time Barbara came home, when we went to the beauty shop together. We know the owner well, and sadly I told Barbara that Roberta's oldest son had been killed in a car accident the preceding week. "I'm not sure if Roberta is back at work yet, Barbara. But if she is, perhaps you had better not talk to her about the accident at all. Her hurt must still be so new and sore." Barbara nodded in agreement, but as she settled into the chair in front of the mirror, I could see her reflected face and knew that she would be unable to contain her feelings. She got up, hugged Roberta, and I heard her say: "You'll miss him, but don't cry. Please don't cry anymore!"

It has always been like that with Barbara. Her sensitivity and perception far outshine her indistinct speech, the shortcomings in her physical coordination, and her inability to read. She is a neat young lady who takes up her full share of space in our family configuration.

Why then does she come home for vacations from a distant city?

Barbara did live home until she was eighteen. Then she, too, wanted to move out like her older sister Karen and brother David, who had left for college. Until recently many young people moved out of our small town after they graduated from high school. Al and I had always known that we might "lose" our children to the big city, for there were few job opportunities on the Mendocino coast unless you wanted to work in the mill or the woods, or become a commercial fisherman.

So it seemed the normal state of affairs for our two older children to leave at eighteen, but it came as somewhat of a shock when our youngest wanted to do the same thing. We had certainly let her become increasingly self-reliant and independent. She, too, had visited friends' homes overnight. She had gone to summer camp and had even spent a week on campus with her sister and brother.

But because she had special needs, because her pattern of growth had been different from that of her brother and sister, we came close to walking into the trap of parental overprotection, which in our case was the illusion of ownership and permanence. Perhaps we thought that she would remain childlike forever and dependent on our everlasting presence. At any rate, she shattered our assumptions with an angry declaration of independence when she was sixteen.

A neighbor of ours had died of cancer. "Uncle" Fay had been a good friend to our children. She couldn't understand that he was gone—why? how? where? We tried to answer her repeated questions until she no longer asked them. A few weeks later she and I were having an angry round-and-round. I nagged. Barbara balked. Suddenly she looked at me and asked, "When are you going to die, Mummy?"

I was shocked. She was worrying about the one life condition that we cannot change for our children with special needs. As I put my arms around her, I assured her that I was feeling fine and should be good for a long, long time. "But why do you ask, Barbara?" Her answer was, "Because then I will be free."

It was the first indication that she viewed us as restraining and oppressive parents. It was her rebellion against being held too close.

The timing was right. I had read about progressive independent living programs in the Scandinavian countries for young adults with mental retardation and wanted to see them with my own eyes. The National Association for Retarded Citizens, an organization of concerned parents and volunteers, supports an annual program of travel grants which enable three or four U.S. citizens to study mental retardation programs abroad and make it possible for those who live abroad to do the same in our country. I sent for an application form and wrote a few letters to inquire about specific names and places in Denmark. That is how I met two persons who were to become significant mentors, coworkers, and friends.

Professor Rosemary Dybwad, in whose honor the grant program was established, took a personal interest in those of us who applied for a stipend. While her husband, Professor Gunnar Dybwad, served as national executive director during the early years of the national association, she had become aware of an amazing phenomenon. Parent groups working on behalf of mentally retarded children were springing up simultaneously in many apparently disconnected parts of the world. To establish links between them, she recruited volunteers who helped her translate newsletters from different languages into English. Soon there was almost no one in the field of mental retardation that she and Gunnar did not know. At the time I applied for the award, Rosemary told me of Robert Perske, a chaplain at the Kansas Neurological Institute, who had just returned from a three-week swing through Denmark, Sweden, and Norway. Perhaps he would share his travel notes with me. Bob turned out to be a generous man to whom the spreading of the word was more important than copyright concerns, and when I had read the diary of his twenty-one day trip and registered the enthusiasm of his voice and long distance phone advice, I knew what I wanted to do. Bob had seen a little bit of everything. I would concentrate on one part of what he had experienced.

Barbara was seventeen when I received the Rosemary Dybwad International Award, and in the fall of 1971 my husband Al, Barbara, her older sister Karen, and I left for Copenhagen. Our twenty-year-old son, David, volunteered to stay at home and supervise our printshop.

Just before we left for the trip, our family had reached

15

an important decision. If it was indeed time for Barbara to leave home, perhaps she should have a little house of her own in which to practice this independence. We cleared an area of our property about a stone's throw from the back porch and began to look at plans. We would start to build when we returned.

Denmark made a tremendous impression on us. Our entire family took a giant step forward in our perception of fine programs for persons with disabilities and our awareness of the growth potential of those who live in such programs.

The day after our arrival in Copenhagen we visited the group home that was to be the core of my study. It was a comfortable three-story brick house on a quiet residential street between two busy boulevards. Twelve young women with moderate mental retardation lived there with their director, three trained care assistants, a full-time cook/housekeeper, and a handyman. Elna Skov, the director, glowed with warmth and enthusiasm. "We would like you to spend some time with us while you are here, Barbara," she told our youngest. "When?" was our daughter's instant reply. We returned to the hotel right then and there to help her pack a small suitcase, and Barbara moved in that day. She spent an entire month at the residence so that I was able to observe and record the goal setting, striving, and "stretching," which are part of the normalization* process, in terms of my own daughter's behavior.

As Al, Karen, and I walked back to our hotel in the evening of that first day, we asked ourselves the big ques-

---

* In 1968 "normalization" was enunciated by Bank-Mikkelsen, director of Danish Mental Retardation Services, as the principle underlying programs for mentally retarded persons and their families.

tion: "How come these girls don't look or act retarded?" A month later we had soaked up enough new concepts, challenging ideas, and food for thought for years to come.

Because Barbara was only a temporary resident and did not know the language, it was decided that she would assist with work around the house instead of "working out" like the other young women. "But," said Elna, turning to Al, "she should learn to walk back and forth to your hotel. You could teach her. First show her the way. Then follow to see that she does it right until she can do it alone."

It was a fifteen-minute walk. Our small town girl had to cross two major boulevards with strange-looking traffic lights (Fort Bragg has only three traffic signals all told!), and she gave her nervous father a couple of scary moments. The first time he walked just a few steps behind her. At corners she would turn around, check for his okay, and then cross alone. The next time he hung back a good distance and let her make her own decision. Sure enough she goofed. He saw her turn left down the big boulevard instead of crossing at the corner. Suddenly she noticed her mistake, but—oh horror!—instead of backtracking to the corner with the signal, she raised her hand like a policeman directing traffic and struck out across the street right in the middle of the block. Al almost had heart failure, but all the speedy little Danish cars stopped in time! Soon she no longer needed anyone's protection. Had she been a regular resident, she would then have been taught a bus route to her place of work.

Shopping came next. I had to admit to Elna that only once in her entire life had Barbara bought a pair of knee socks for herself, all by herself. Elna's residents gradually learned to purchase everything they needed independently. Much staff time was expended to teach them about quality, good value, and good style. They took great pride in their purchases and appearance, and without exception everyone looked neat, stylish, and appropriately dressed.

I asked Elna if she and her staff would write a program for Barbara "as if she were a Danish girl entering as a new resident." She looked at me quizzically and asked, "Wouldn't your feelings be hurt?" I assured her that I could take it, and she and her assistants promptly sat down with Barbara and prepared a one-month program:

> Not to suck her thumb.
> To keep shoulders back.
> Not to laugh too loud or without motivation.
> To sit down on chairs gently and in a ladylike manner.
> To eat less noisily at the table.
> To keep her blouse all the way out or in and to arrange the collar of her coat neatly.

The goals were simple, straightforward, and attainable. All of us—Barbara, staff persons, and family—evaluated her progress at the end of the month.

We began to respect the idea of risk taking which Bob Perske had experienced and vividly described in his travel reports. It was obvious that Barbara's coordination and mobility were improving. At home our awkward, fearful girl hardly ever walked up and down stairs. California homes tend to be the one-story, rambling ranchstyle variety. Here she was learning to negotiate the steep winding staircase to her third-floor bedroom. Before the month was over, she could do it without holding on to the banister, even while carrying something in her hands. It was simply taken for granted that she would learn. For many young people in Danish programs, risk taking was part of a work situation in which the use of expensive power tools required concentration and resulted in great poise. We also noted that continued education motivated them to strengthen their independent living skills.

Money was spent generously on many programs. Persons who were unable to walk were provided with staff and equipment to put them on their feet. Furnishings in state residences and in community group homes were almost luxurious by our standards. They seemed to say, "Nothing is too good for you," and the young men and women who lived surrounded by such beauty grew in pride and care for their possessions.

We soon realized that excellent staff training—both academic and practical training for front line personnel —was one of the secrets of success for programs and residents. The positive, dynamic attitudes of well-trained staff persons reflected directly on residents, increasing their self-confidence and enhancing their self-concept.

The Danes, too, were concerned with the issue of parental overprotection. I was apparently not the only mother in the world who bought all her teenage daughter's clothes for her! Elna told me of mothers who answered for their children, pre-empted their every decision, and never discussed with them the implication of their condition on their adult life in the community.

As I sorted through and assessed my experiences, one thought surfaced that depressed me. How could I ever "sell" all these beautiful concepts at home? "Of course!" they would snort, "that's what you get in a socialist country." It happened otherwise.

I had promised Bob Perske, newly arrived in Omaha, Nebraska, to direct the Greater Omaha Association for the Retarded, that I would stop and report on my experiences. "I think I'm too tired to come, Bob," I said when I phoned him from New York. "Besides, I have a cold, and next week is Thanksgiving, and I want to fly straight home."

"I wish you'd come, Lotte," he said earnestly. "I really wish you'd take a couple of extra days to see what's happening here. This is even more exciting than Denmark."

With that he brought me up short. Coming from the man who had first introduced me to all the exciting Scandinavian normalization ideas, it had to be true.

And it was. It was actually happening in conservative, cornbelt Nebraska. ENCOR, the Eastern Nebraska Community Office of Retardation, was putting together a comprehensive, community-based program for children and adults, which included former institutional residents and children with severe multiple developmental disabilities. I no longer needed to be depressed about our country's long distance from Denmark and socialism. We could make good programs happen here at home.

It was high time, for our cheerful child was becoming a grouchy teenager. At first we thought she was suffering from an acute attack of "circusitis," the dread disease that overcomes people who have had too good a time at parties or on vacation. "She'll get over it," we thought. But she did not. Every morning it was a struggle to get her off to school on time. After years of yearning to be allowed to ride the yellow school bus, she now complained about riding "with all the little kids." She balked at going to her separate special school. "Why can't I go to junior high?" she wanted to know. Finally she announced in total rebellion: "I hate Fort Bragg! I hate home!"

That did it. We scrapped the idea of building a halfway house in our own backyard and began to plan for her move out of town.

It has not been all smooth sailing either for Barbara or for us. Her first placement in a brand-new family care home in a neighboring county collapsed when the caretaker turned out to be a person with alcoholism. The next placement—with the parents of a schoolmate—was excellent but had to be temporary. After that she spent four years in a large city in a residence within close reach of her brother and sister who were working and attending college nearby. She was contented at first, but when Karen and David moved away, she felt bereft.

It hurt us to hear our daughter say, "I wanna come closer to home," when we had no choices of quality living arrangements in our rural area. After spending a weekend with us, she would drag her heels at bus time until we almost missed it. I felt like gathering her into my arms and saying, "Stay home, girl. Come back and stay with Mom and Dad."

But that is not the answer, we know. For, at twenty-six she still has a lifetime ahead of her and is young enough to grow and develop and learn.

Each time she returns home we have an opportunity to take a fresh look at her and to marvel at the progress she has made. In more ways than one she is a well-rounded person who never looks the same. She is about five foot seven and "over-weighs" at about a hundred and eighty pounds. With her motherly, hourglass shape she takes after Al's mother and sister. Karen and I envy her waist and hips, for we tend to be flat in the bustle and over-endowed on top. Barbara is the only blond in a family of brunettes. Her eyes are bright blue and her nose short and straight, while our eyes range from grey blue to dark.

When Barbara is well rested, interested, and happy, you probably won't notice that she has any problem at all until she speaks. Her language is basic and meaningful, and in spite of short-cut sentences and fuzzy consonants she usually persists until she has made her point. When she is tired, bored, or angry she sticks her thumb in her mouth, rounds her shoulders, and bends over as if she were leaning on it. On happy days her smile is radiant and her expression and touch alive, light, and loving.

It's her walking and running that look weird and give her trouble. Her flat feet turn outward, and when she breaks into a run, her arms swing wildly and she bends over at the waist. Her coordination has definitely worsened since childhood. Too many tumbles have made her more and more fearful. When she was in her teens, she slipped on a small rug and broke her leg. Crutches were a challenge that summer, but she learned to use them and healed. Soon afterwards, she fell and badly wrenched her knee, and that has become a long-range handicap much like a football injury. For the past five years she has had to wear braces on both her lower legs, first to support the wobbly knee and now both her ankles. The braces are made of steel and leather and are attached to husky, high-top boots. She puts them on faithfully most mornings, although she occasionally sneaks a day off and wears tennis shoes. So she wears long pants almost always and long dresses for formal occasions. Barbara likes clothes. She knows what she wants to wear, and she can look neatly put together when she remembers to tuck in and smooth down blouse tails and coat collars.

So Barbara comes and goes. Slowly but surely we have watched her become more and more responsible, independent, and assertive. She will probably always lag behind her so-called "normal" friends and relations, but with acceptance of her differentness and support of her efforts to learn, we hope that she will continue to strengthen the skills and abilities with which she can control her environment. Her greater independence from us is the best insurance for her future. We are trying to prepare her for a future without us, one for which she will be equipped not only with practical survival skills, but also with essential emotional strengths.

Like the adult that she now is, Barbara lives away from us, her parents. But as a beloved and welcome daughter, she returns often for weekends, holidays, and vacations. She joins us for occasional trips and joyfully spends time with her brother and sister wherever they may be.

One time when I was writing and searching for an apt definition of "home," I asked Barbara: "What do you think a good home is, Barbara? How would you describe one?" She thought and replied, "Home is a moving out." Barbara has indeed grown up. We have all grown with her. How it happened is in this book.

2 *Retrospect*

ALL OF OUR CHILDREN WERE much wanted. Like so many post-World War II couples, Al and I planned to have three or four. Barbara was the third and last. In spite of her problem called mental retardation, she grew up to be a fully three-dimensional member of our family—not a diagnosis or a label, but a human being first and foremost. Our family was sometimes small, often extended, and we functioned with all of our tensions and mutual supports, against the backdrop of a small northern California town.

We have known sad and happy times, angry and funny moments. Quiet conferences for two in the bedroom, and noisy discussions around the dining room table for a dozen. We weren't always in harmony, but we have come through as a family of individuals who care.

My husband's name is Al—Alfred H. Moise, Jr., to be exact. The *H* stands for "Huger" after a confederate general and friend of the family. Al's family roots go into the genteel South of New Orleans and Alabama, and the rest of us wish that we knew more about them. Al's father died long ago. I never had a chance to meet him, but his mother, Eva, lived to the ripe old age of ninety-three and was an important grandmother figure. We called her

"Mud," a respectful carryover from Al's childhood when he had trouble pronouncing the *th* in mother.

Al was born in New Rochelle, New York. His father was a pioneer in the electrical world. As a young man, Al, Sr., helped wire the Statue of Liberty and installed the searchlight on the battleship *Maine*. Later he became a cameraman in the budding U.S. movie industry. When he was invited to shoot films in Europe the family packed up, and the two children, Al and Grace, spent several years in boarding schools in England, while their parents lived in France and Switzerland. Al was twelve when the family returned home and moved to southern California, where he graduated from Glendale High School a year after John Wayne. The yearbook documents the fact that "Duke Morrison" played on the football team while our Al belonged to the Latin Club! He was not quite sixteen when he graduated, shortly before The Great Depression.

A lot happened to him during the nineteen years until we met in 1946. He worked in a blueprint shop in Los Angeles, hopped up cars with his best friend Dave, sold Fuller Brush products, and was married in 1933 to Babe Bell. Four hours after their son was born in 1934, Babe died of a hemorrhage. Al named the baby after himself and his father.

It was rough for Al for a long time afterwards. He could not take care of a baby and work. Grandpa Al was having traumatic surgery for a detached retina, and so young Al went to live with his maternal grandparents—the Bells— in Enderlin, North Dakota. Al visited his son when he could manage it, which was not very often, and I am still amazed at how much father and son resemble each other—even in habits and mannerisms—with so little time spent together. The Bells were railroaders. Their youngest was still a child when the baby came to them, and they provided a warm, loving home for little Al. During World War II they moved to Fullerton, California.

More than anything else, Al wanted to take part in raising his child, but it didn't work out that way. He married again, hoping for a home for young Al, but divorced his wife shortly before World War II. Then he sold his service station and entered the navy and since young Al had never really known any other home than that of his grandparents, everyone agreed that it would be best if they adopted him. Thus young Al became Alfred Charles Bell. He is now married and the father of a lovely young daughter. He and his family live in California, and we feel a warm kinship with them.

I guess I'm next. I'm Lotte Ella Moise, and I could get carried away talking about my family because I know a lot more about them than Al does about his. My first name is really the tail end of Charlotte, but my parents liked simple, short names, so Lotte it is. Ella was the name of my father's mother.

I was born in Duesseldorf, Germany, towards the end of World War I. Looking back I feel that the historical reality of having a partially Jewish ancestry in that time and place gave me an added strength and resilience without which I might not have been able to overcome the "borning" of a disabled child.

My parents were Kurt and Minnie Bardach. Kurt was a physician who specialized in dermatology. In his day this included venereal diseases, and much of his work consisted of counseling with such patients. The miracle of penicillin had not yet happened, and syphilis and gonorrhea cast lifelong shadows on those who contracted them. "Papi," as we called him, worked especially well with young people, and I remember his speaking with pride of a suicidal patient whom he helped to piece together a life which had seemed shattered.

Papi's father had also been a physician and divided his practice between a spa in southern Germany and the elegant French Riviera, so the entire family spoke French as well as German. Grandma Ella, I was told, was vain, attractive, and flirted with men. She and Grandpa were divorced after they had one daughter, but later they remarried each other and had two more children. Papi used to say that he was a child of his parents' second marriage and confused everybody. The story goes that the divorce was caused by my grandfather's heavy gambling habit and that their second venture included a rather airtight property agreement so that Grandma Ella's income did not depend on the fluctuations of his luck.

I hardly remember my grandfather, but I have interesting recollections of Grandma Ella's stormy visits. She was a demanding woman who managed to disrupt childhood routines delightfully. She would insist that my brother Henry and I did not need naps when she visited us and then promptly dozed off in an armchair, leaving us bored and sleepy.

My mother Minnie was a beautiful wife, homemaker, and mother. "Nana" had no major interests outside the family, so I have good memories of time spent with her. We would have been happy and carefree if it had not been for the long shadow of my mother's periodic "nervous breakdowns," which were really whopping depressions. Even in our medically enlightened circle of friends, these were considered sort of embarrassing, and I was scared to death whenever my bright, energetic mother underwent one of her depressive episodes. We suffered with her for many, many years.

Nana's parents lived in a large rambling house a few blocks from ours, and both of them provided total back-up for Henry and me in times of sickness or trouble. "Opa" Freundlich was tall and handsome with a handle-bar mustache. He was a baker's son from a small town in southern Germany. He had left home early, apprenticed himself to a machinist in a nearby town, and became one of the pioneers in the German refrigeration industry. He had also taught himself mathematics and chemistry and impressed us children immensely by his ability to multiply in his head. He could do three digits by three digits while we were still writing down the numbers!

"Oma" was small and roly-poly. She tended to be brusque and to say "no" and then do "yes," and when she was excited, her false teeth made a clicking sound. Once when Henry and I were staying with her and Opa, we hid her dentures, which stood in a glass by her bedside. Boy, did we get it! People sometimes said that I resembled Oma, intending it as a compliment, but I was secretly terrified that I might grow up to look like her. Yet I loved her, and I can still smell the freshness of her cologne and remember how snug I felt in their house.

Both Oma and Opa were pillars of Duesseldorf's Reform Jewish community. Henry and I grew up as Lutherans, and when I began confirmation classes, I had many questions about the difference between Christianity and Judaism. I asked childish questions and received simple answers, but I felt quite comfortable about the process that helped me to integrate the different traditions of my parents' families.

As a child, I felt that I was an important person to those

around me. My mother thought I was. She took me for walks. She stayed home in the afternoon to help me with homework, and sometimes I sat on her lap.

My father thought so, too. He insisted that I be dressed up when we all went to the cafe on Saturday afternoons, and he helped me with math homework, which he knew how to do better than my mother did. After he had solved a problem for me, he sometimes tore up the paper and said, "Now go do it yourself. You can do it." I sat on his lap, too, and on mornings when there was no school I crawled into their bed.

Maria was our cook and maid. She sometimes bawled me out and even spanked me occasionally, but she more than made up for it by taking me to her family's farm on her days off. There I drank goat's milk, used an outhouse, and learned to ride a bike.

My brother Henry was four years younger than I, and I thought he was a brat. I bossed him around, so I'm sure he thought I was important.

I was somebody when I went downtown, too. My parents sent me on errands, and when the merchant asked for a delivery address, I would say, "Duisburgerstrasse 134—the big yellow house," and he'd reply, "Oh, you must be Doktor Bardach's little girl," and I would feel proud and respected.

I wasn't always on top of the world, of course. I longed to be thinner and much taller. I envied a girl in my class who could actually sit on her pigtails, while my own wavy hair barely made it to the collar. I was lousy at gym and didn't score high on sex appeal. At age thirteen none of the boys even looked at me when we strolled down the town's main boulevard to check out "the scenery," but overall I had a good life.

29

Changes came gradually. One day I was a protected, respected, happy-go-lucky *Backfisch* (a German expression for teenagers literally meaning "fish yet to be baked"); the next day I felt troubled.

Troubles certainly didn't come overnight. Germany after World War I was in constant turmoil. Many private homes were still occupied by French troops years after the war. My grandparents had soldiers living in their large three-story house for many years. These men were enemies to us, and I was afraid of them. A French officer was billeted in our own living room until my little brother was born, and we were permitted to reclaim it. Maria was indignant because this so-called "gentleman" had spit cherry pits on the rug, and his orderly left black boot marks all over the hardwood floors.

I did not understand the galloping inflation, but I do remember Papi rushing up the stairs from his office, clutching a few bills, and shouting to my mother that she must go out at once to buy something. It could not wait until later because the money would be worthless by evening. I also vaguely remember the Spartakist uprisings when left-wing and right-wing political party members fought in the streets, and we boarded over the windows on the street floor.

All of these heavy political happenings had not touched my feeling of self-worth. That began with the emergence of Nazism. First there were parades of brown-shirted men with red, white, and black swastika armbands, band music, and raised arm salutes. It took years before I was able to enjoy brass bands again, and I still jump when I suddenly see a swastika. Radio speeches by a man named Hitler seemed to upset all the grownups. I heard whispered talk about Jewish people and Communist party members disappearing in concentration camps. In the evening my parents huddled around the radio with doors and windows shut. They listened to news from foreign stations just across the border. It was strictly *verboten*, they told me, and my heart was heavy with the secret of our common danger.

School continued to be a happy place. Our headmistress was a feisty lady who refused to tolerate nonsense, regardless of whether it was initiated by the students or the new bureaucracy. But even she was unable to stop the changes that steamrolled over us all. All of a sudden there were new biology textbooks full of discussions about "race." The words "Aryan," "Gentile," and "Nordic" became part of the new vocabulary that had to be learned. Once we were able to play a trick on a handsome new biology teacher. We asked him to pick out the most Nordic-looking girl in our class, and he pointed to my blond friend, Ruth, whose mother was Jewish!

Like a one-two blow the sky fell in on me in two installments. The first blow was delivered by one of my best friends. She was a mature girl, older looking than her age, and very well read. She took me aside in the schoolyard one day and asked if I was worried.

"Worried? Why should I be worried?" I dodged.

"Don't you even read what's going on?" she wanted to know.

"I have way too much homework."

"You're sure hiding your head in the sand," she commented and pressed on about Hitler's book, *Mein Kampf*, and how he seemed to be carrying out that program chapter by chapter.

"But nobody's doing anything to *me!*" I protested.

"Not yet," she said, and walked away.

The next blow came in a letter. For years I had looked forward to joining my father's tennis club, and now that I was fourteen I was eligible for a junior membership. The Red and White Club returned my application with regret. By edict of Herr Kultur Minister Goebbels all German sports activities must be racially purified. I had never felt so crushed.

A few days later I decided to visit my "Onkel Doktor." A slow-speaking, scholarly gentleman with a white goatee and twinkly eyes, he was the brother of my Jewish grandfather.

"Onkel Doktor, I'd like you to take a drop of my blood and let me see it under the microscope," I told him.

"But why, Lotte? Don't you feel well?"

"I feel okay. I just want to see how my blood is different from everybody else's."

He laughed, hugged me, and tried to assure me that all this talk about blood and races was scientific hocus-pocus and political nonsense, but somehow he failed to comfort me where it really hurt. Hitler's Germany had already told me that I was "lesser than."

I left Germany to finish high school in England the following year, and my apprenticeship at hurt feelings continued for a while. I was, of course, aware of the dangers I had escaped in Germany, but it was difficult being a foreigner in a strange land. I had to master English, learn how to use different coins, weights, and measures, catch up with new school subjects, digest suet pudding, and play field hockey. The worst times were at night when the dormitory lights were turned out. Jokes that I could not yet understand bounced over my head from bed to bed, while I soaked homesick tears into my clammy pillow.

We "trickled" across the Atlantic one by one during

the year 1937. Papi went first in order to establish himself as a duly certified and licensed physician in New York State. Nana had to pack and wind up the forced sale of our beautiful house in Duesseldorf. Henry finished school in England and followed during the summer. I graduated from Charlotte Mason College in December and experienced a stormy winter crossing on the good old H.M.S. *Berengaria.* By Christmas we were reunited in Flushing, New York.

At first living in the United States was difficult, for this was still Depression time. Nana became my father's office nurse and receptionist. Although we counted patients for a long time, we didn't go hungry and learning to live frugally was an almost exhilarating experience. Henry graduated from Flushing High School, was drafted into the army, and later became an economist who now works as a U.S. Foreign Service Officer. I gave up my childhood dream of studying medicine once and for all and tackled the employment market of New York City—first as a teacher and later as a personnel and guidance counselor.

I was eager to tackle my new life in America, but it wasn't as easy as I had thought. The young woman who had proudly graduated from college with honors in England was once more a nobody in New York. The teaching credential turned out not to be worth two years of American college credits. My British accent stuck out like a sore thumb. My clothes looked dowdy, and my figure was too ample. I was a greenhorn refugee and felt awful.

I had to start all over again to establish my "somebodiness." I took more courses and searched for career direction. I hated my first teaching job but stuck to it for one year. I was young and healthy, and with my family's loving support life began to look up. When I became part of the local dating scene, my shaky self-image settled down comfortably.

The beginning of World War II made me wish fervently that I could help our new country. Ever since I was a small child, history seemed to have been made right in my own backyard, and though I feared war and passionately wished for peace, I knew that I had to become involved.

This war was different. This war was partially directed against Hitler's Germany and would surely be the last. When I became a citizen of the United States in 1944, I was pleased that I would finally be able to enter government service. I interrupted college work to enter the Women's Reserve of the Coast Guard, because this was the only branch of all the military services that seemed to serve a useful peacetime purpose. I became a SPAR, an acronym which stands for the Coast Guard motto, *Semper Paratus* ("Always Ready") or, in our vernacular, "A Spar is what a sailor clings to in distress!"

SPARs trained at the Coast Guard Academy in New London, Connecticut, under the amused stares of male reserve officers. We survived miles of marching and hours of drilling. We almost killed ourselves and each other learning to handle a lifeboat on the Thames River, struggled with plane and ship recognition, and learned to turn out wrinkle-free beds and dust-free rooms. For many years I amazed friends and family by my ability to undress, pop in and out of a shower, and dress again in five minutes flat!

We graduated in 1944—the last class to do so and thus we were forever frozen in our lofty rank of ensigns—and were sent to the four winds to help our male counterparts Win The War. In order to avoid being cooped up in a de-

34

coding room at headquarters in Washington, D.C., I had indicated that I did not want to use my knowledge of German. I preferred to use my counseling and personnel skills in faraway places, perhaps the West Coast. Visions of warm waves and palm trees. I was ordered to Port Angeles, Washington.

My two years of military service were a rich experience. I learned to love the Olympic Peninsula, Vancouver Island, and our West Coast. I wrestled with the human needs of sixty young SPARs in my charge in the constricting, confining, and unbending military framework and hammered out tenuous working relationships with salty seadogs who really didn't understand or appreciate women in uniform. I began to test my own strengths and principles, and it took a year before my quarterly fitness report, which had nothing to do with health, reflected respect growing between the commanding officer of the base and myself. I learned much about people from all walks of life and all corners of our country. The work was exciting and a challenge, but when the war ended, most of us were ready and eager to return home to shape the peace, our lives, and our wardrobes.

I met Al when I was in Seattle, decommissioning the SPAR barracks, which were located in an old-fashioned hotel. One evening when I came out of my office into the lobby, I saw a tall, handsome sailor teasing Nell, our switchboard operator/receptionist. "Lotte, meet Al!" she said, avoiding any reference to my rank or duty officer position and thus giving me a chance to chat with this guy without the usual officer-enlisted constraints which plagued our social lives.

By the end of the evening a half dozen disorganized facts and impressions about Al rattled around in my head.

He was a radioman first class and had seen a lot of action in Europe. His ship was just now being decommissioned at the Seattle Navy Base. He was divorced and had a son. He seemed intelligent, funny, and warm, and I knew that I wanted to see more of him.

Our courtship was pretty one-sided. Al claims that I chased him from one Seattle bar to another. He was obviously enjoying himself and avoiding commitments. I never could figure out if I was making any headway at all among the girls that he squired around Seattle.

A few weeks later when we had both been discharged, I spent a weekend with him in Long Beach. We swam and talked and necked under his mother's appraising and watchful eyes, and I fell totally in love. It seemed like a hopeless situation. I was en route to Mexico City to spend the summer studying Spanish. Al wanted to visit a friend and former shipmate in Fort Bragg on the Mendocino coast. Together they planned to venture north to Fairbanks, Alaska.

We wrote a lot of letters that year. I had returned to New York to my parents' home and to an interesting job and many good friends. A year later, in 1947, both Al and I felt that we needed to give our brief romance and long correspondence a road test, and he hitchhiked down the Alaska Highway to meet me. He offered to come to New York, but I needed to work out this big decision away from the comfort of my family's home. It was the first time in my life that my father was boycotting one of my actions. It was a gentle boycott. He said little to oppose me, but he offered no financial aid for his daughter's "Go West" venture to meet an ex-sailor who lived in a small cabin in Fairbanks and did janitorial work. I took a leave of absence and invested in a railroad ticket to Seattle. Al and

I put all of our combined money into the purchase of a Coast Guard surplus jeep and headed north. We arrived in Fairbanks broke, happy, and ready to get married.

Al's vision of having a full-time *hausfrau* for a wife did not last long. We needed money to pay for a lot, a tiny fourteen-by twenty-foot cabin, and minimum furnishings. By the time we moved into this snug little home, it hardly challenged my nesting instinct. Al returned to his janitor contracts, and I found a secretarial job with the arctic Naval Petroleum Reserve.

We were a working couple for two years before we became parents. First we took another trip "outside" so that Al could meet my parents and receive their retroactive blessing. It was on that swing down the California coast in 1948 that I first came to Fort Bragg. There just happened to be some property for sale on Sherwood Road. The two-acre lot was graced by beautiful redwoods, and it came with a view of the Noyo River. We kept thinking and talking about this land as we continued our vacation and finally decided that we had to check it out on our way north, to find out if we could afford it.

In a roundabout way that is how Karen came to be. She was conceived on the Mendocino coast on our northbound detour and was bumped and bounced in utero over the rough, dusty Alaska Highway as we returned to Fairbanks in our open jeep. She was born in St. Joseph's Hospital on the banks of the Chena River on my mother's birthday in 1949. "Chena," her middle name, stands for pleasant waters. We wanted our sourdough child to have a proper souvenir of Alaska while it was still a territory.

In September of that year we packed our belongings into the jeep. This time it had a cover on it. Karen travelled in a specially adapted folding bathinette between the front seats. She was exactly four months old when we turned south to our land on Sherwood Road in Fort Bragg, California.

David followed two years later. He was an indirect result of our country's Korean "police action" of 1950–1952. We had just settled into our new house in Fort Bragg when Al, who was still in the inactive reserve, received orders to return to the navy. Since Karen was only a year old it seemed early to start another baby, but I had sad premonitions of being a lonely widow with an only child. We also wondered if we might not be too old for another baby by the time Al returned. David was born in New York City, where Karen and I were staying with my parents while Al served on Guam.

After Al's return in the spring of 1952, we drove home to Fort Bragg in a 1926 Rolls Royce, which we had purchased for five hundred dollars from a Park Avenue dowager. It was a shiny, elegant limousine with ample room for a portacrib for David and a sleeping bag for Karen, who called it "my house." We meandered cross-country with laundry lines slung across the back and suitcases packed on the running boards. Six years later when we needed money to add on to our house, we sold the car for fifteen hundred dollars. David has never quite forgiven us.

It felt good to come home. All the way across country three-year-old Karen had insisted on crawling into her sleeping bag wherever we stayed overnight. It had become her security blanket. We drove into our yard late one night on our return. As we bundled her into her crib, she woke up and asked, "Is this my bed?" and when we nodded, she wriggled out of her bag and under the covers contentedly.

Our small house was warm and comfortable and so was

our marriage. Just before the Korean War interrupted our lives and plans, Al had begun working with a young printer and hoped to continue his apprenticeship with him. I had no particular plans beyond motherhood. We hoped to have three or four children and let the future take care of itself.

3 Fort Bragg, California?

FORT BRAGG IS A SMALL town on the Mendocino coast in northern California—*not* in North Carolina.

In 1950 nobody had even heard of Fort Bragg or Mendocino County. While Al was overseas and I was staying with my folks in New York, I would occasionally see an attractive household item and send it to our house. And when we were getting ready to drive home in the old Rolls Royce, I lugged sizeable parcels of accumulated children's treasures to the Flushing post office.

"You must be mistaken, Ma'am!" was the inevitable preamble from the man behind the counter. "There's a Fort Bragg in North Carolina—the army base," he would say as he pushed the package back towards me.

I pushed back. "No, I *mean* California. Fort Bragg, California. We live there."

He protested again.

"But we have a house there, right on Sherwood Road!" I was beginning to wish that I had a picture of it to show to this man. He was clearly getting irritated at my doubting his postal authority. "Couldn't you look it up?"

He grumbled and disappeared behind a pile of mail sacks. When he returned, he was carrying a large directory. As he plunked it punishingly on the counter, he asked, "Now between where and where did you say this place is?"

"North of San Francisco and south of Eureka—just about halfway, and on the ocean."

He adjusted his glasses and ran his finger slowly down a column of fine print. "You're right! Here it is. Never heard of the place before!"

At the receiving end of the postal process, we simply assumed that many of our letters would take longer than usual to reach us. We told our friends to be sure to write out "California," to write it in red, to write it in capitals, to underline it. Even so, limp, tired-looking letters arrived with "Not N.C." scrawled impatiently across the front.

Our visitors had problems getting to Fort Bragg, too. They would look at a map of California and conclude that we were a hop, skip, and a jump from San Francisco. They were fooled. The roads curved and twisted even more than they do now. "Better allow five and a half to six hours," we'd tell them. Nowadays we cover the same one hundred seventy miles in little more than half the time, though we still drive our roads with respect.

Fort Bragg is located just about halfway between the San Francisco Bay area and the Oregon border. Its small harbor, called Noyo, offers the only shelter to boats along this entire length of rugged coastline, and the Coast Guard cutter keeps busy the year around. The population of the incorporated city has not substantially changed in many years. It is still about five thousand, but Fort Bragg's days of sleepy isolation were over long ago.

Our small acreage on Sherwood Road is two miles inland, where the coastal fog gives way to sunshine in the late mornings. When winter storms roughen the ocean and the wind stands right, we can open a west window and listen to the roar. We look out over the Noyo River valley, and a tunnel for the "Skunk" train line pierces our hillside. The line takes its name from its original self-propelled cars with gas engines. "You can smell them before you see them," the old-timers used to say.

Fishermen call the area "Tunnel Hill" and use an old trail across our property to reach the railroad trestle and their favorite fishing holes. Our children knew every fishing hole along the river, and when they learned to swim, we let them go to Bear Butte (they thought it was "Bare Butt") with their friends. The height of danger, they now tell us, were the times when they dared each other to stand with their tummies tucked in and holding their breath in the small cut-out places inside the tunnel while the train rumbled through.

Our house is built of redwood and surrounded by them. Whenever we cut wood for the stove or clear some land to let the sunshine in, it is a carefully reached decision. In this climate trees and people need space and sunlight.

In spite of its name, Fort Bragg's military history was brief and uneventful. All of it happened in the year 1857 when Lt. Horatio Gibson came with a contingent of National Guardsmen and established a post to cope with an alleged Indian problem. The Pomos, however, spent their time fishing and weaving beautiful baskets rather than making war, so the troops withdrew. Lieutenant Gibson named the spot Fort Bragg in honor of his former commanding officer, who happened to be the same General Braxton Bragg of Fort Bragg, North Carolina, fame.

Many of the people who originally settled on the Mendocino coast came from Finland, Italy, and Portugal.

The Finns knew lumbering and sheep raising, and the Italians and Portuguese were experienced fishermen. These were Fort Bragg's chief support activities when we first came here. Our neighbors on Tunnel Hill were mainly Finnish. Names like Oija, Kinnunen, and Korhonen lilted melodiously over the six-party telephone line, and we soon learned that they took neighborliness seriously. Uncle Ed to the west of us and Uncle Fay to the east decided that it would be too dangerous for Karen and David to walk to their houses along the road. Too many big logging trucks. They helped us clear a trail and build steps over the fence so that our children could come and go safely on errands and visits to their homes.

We had chosen to live in Fort Bragg because of its beauty and because both Al and I wanted to raise our children in a friendly small town. "What is Al going to *do*?" our friends would ask, after we had explained the puzzle of our location. We had no real worries. Any job would be okay with Al, who was used to working hard with his hands. He returned to the little printshop in which he had apprenticed before the Korean War. The owners patiently taught him what they knew, and he was a quick learner.

It was love at first sight between Al and the presses, the paper and ink, the balance and design of words on a page, the customers and their causes, even the precariously balanced mountain of papers on his desk. When Karen and David complained about their father's endless hours at the shop, I explained that he was there to make money for us all until they believed he printed it. At first we ate a lot of beans and surplus surf fish donated by friends, but for many years now Redwood Coast Printers has been our own business, including the antique wooden

43

building on Main Street which survived the 1906 earth-
quake and has a slightly rakish tilt to it. According to
Al, it is the town that leans! Tourists marvel at the
"McGovern For President" sign which he stubbornly
refused to remove in personal protest against the elec-
tion of President Nixon. Many times over the years Al the
Printer has run his presses to help me get out the word
about my new insights and experiences.

Our house was in apple-pie order when we returned
home in 1952. I threw myself energetically into the
business of being a good mother and countrywoman. The
hardwood floors and windows of the house on Tunnel Hill
sparkled. Since the women in the neighborhood were
fantastic cooks, my own repertoire expanded by a recipe
a day. The fragrance of Finnish sweet bread or sourdough
rye often greeted visitors to my kitchen, and I began to
take a squirrely pride in seeing my rows of glass jars full
of spiced pears, cucumber pickles, chutney, and berry
jam. Summertime became a series of harvesting expedi-
tions up and down our road, as Karen pulled her little red
wagon and I pushed David in the stroller.

Fort Bragg surprised us with its indoor, heated municipal swimming pool built during WPA days. That's where
I applied my first volunteer energies. I put my Red Cross
water safety instructor's certificate to work and taught
summer swim classes to five-year-olds. The PTA enlisted
me before our children were even enrolled in school, and
the Lutheran pastor was delighted to introduce a
German-speaking person to his overwhelmingly Finnish
congregation. I also put my name on the substitute
teachers' list. In spite of Grandma Mud's dire prediction
that this town would be way too quiet, I was finding
plenty to do.

I could never have managed any of these activities without my neighbors' offers to help me with babysitting. Olga, Ve, Sylvia, and Eileen were strong women—kind but firm—and wonderfully skilled in parenting. The children were in good hands on the occasional days when I was called to school. There I made an indelible impression, not because of my superior teaching skills, but because I arrived in our stately old Rolls Royce.

Although we were relatively isolated from California's major tourist attractions, we began to have many visitors in our home. Aunt Martha, my father's energetic sister, was one of our first guests and a particularly memorable one. She was a busy physician and quite a globetrotter during her vacations, who decided that she would fly to Little River, the airport fifteen miles south of us.

The Little River airport has always been a problem of sorts. Legend has it that a young lieutenant was sent to Mendocino early in World War II to select a likely site for an emergency airstrip. He conducted his investigation from the shelter of one of our inns, where he could huddle close to the bar to ward off the chilly summer fog. It was there that he was told of a fine, level location in Little River. The runway that resulted is level, all right. It's a paved strip 5,250 feet long, free of all visual obstructions except fog—cool, low-slung, frequent fog. The various small commercial airlines that have tried to establish regular schedules to the coast from time to time have all pulled out after a few months because, they say, the operation doesn't pay.

Aunt Martha, however, had discovered this obscure air connection and announced that she would fly to Little River. We drove to meet her. I remember the preparations. I even remember the matching royal blue terry cloth suits in which I dressed Karen and David. Al shined up the Rolls Royce. I poured myself into a panty girdle in order to smooth out the telltale bulge of our third child. You would have to know Aunt Martha to understand why I did this. She had been an insightful, important advisor to me at certain crossroads of my adolescent and young adult life. I had consulted her during Al's and my correspondence courtship. I valued her advice and had learned to parry her often bluntly honest comments. Our chosen lifestyle ran somewhat counter to hers. She was about to meet us on our own turf for the first time, and I was just a little afraid of running straight into an argument about the wisdom of having another child when we were still so poor by her standards. The age factor—I was thirty-five that year—did not cross my mind.

Anyway, I wore the girdle, the fog rolled in, and we were told that the plane would not land in Little River that day. Meanwhile somewhere above us, the flight crew were getting a taste of Aunt Martha at her best. She had a fit when they told her that the coast was fogged in and that she would have to get off in Ukiah, 55 miles short of her destination. She refused to get off, and only the cool announcement that she was welcome to ride to the end of their run, one hundred fifty miles north of Fort Bragg, convinced her to disembark. Al, the children, and I drove from the cool of the fog into the intense heat of the valley to meet her. The Rolls Royce registered its disapproval by overheating shortly before cresting Seven Mile Hill. The kids were crabby and impatient, and I was hot.

We had a fine visit anyway, and my pregnancy proceeded without a hitch. In those days we were "delicate" about such natural conditions as pregnancy, and teachers were not encouraged to continue working in day school once their pregnancy became obvious. As a result, I shifted my activities from daytime substituting to teaching a night school class in English and citizenship for the foreign born.

The adult class was a marvelous experience in "special" education. Because there was little published material available, I had to improvise. Lessons tended to revolve around the students' daily experiences. They wanted to learn the words they needed for working in the mill or as domestic helpers. Many of my elderly students had had little opportunity for formal schooling in the countries they came from and possessed limited reading and writing skills in their own language. They were still firmly rooted in the Finnish, Italian, Portuguese, or German of their youth, and English was the hard-learned language of their middle years. Together we overcame many a "communications deficit."

I gave little homework and no tests at all, and yet I knew that the students were learning. Their steady attendance on rainy nights after a long working day impressed me. They seemed to look at night school not only as a place to study, but also as an occasion for social gathering, a source of mutual moral support, and general counseling. It began to dawn on me that the nonacademic aspects of the class were contributing as much, if not more, to the acquisition of language, as the formal lesson materials. This special piece of learning I remembered and welcomed a few years later when I became a special education teacher.

The class members surprised me by turning their 1953 Christmas party into a baby shower for me, and they invited Al and the children.

Karen and David had taken my pregnancy in stride. Al

and I gave them as much factual information as they seemed to understand or ask for. They liked putting their hands on my middle and feeling the baby move. We had lots of friends in various stages of expectancy, and in October our good friend, Edith, gave birth to her third child, Keith. So the children were pretty blasé about the whole thing. The class party—close to the anticipated birth of the baby, the arrival of Grandma Mud, and of Christmas—seemed to quicken the pace of their expectancy. I went home on vacation to keep the home front calm and coordinated and to prepare for the birth of our third child.

Barbara was born December 11, 1953, in the old Redwood Coast Hospital.

4 *Third Children Are Easy*

I WAS AN OLD HAND AT coming home with a baby. Four days in the hospital had given me a fine rest. My stitches felt okay, and I was able to get into my grey wool skirt with only a slightly deeper than usual breath.

Karen and David were wildly excited about their baby sister, and Grandma Mud had been impatiently staying with us for more than a week. I was more concerned with keeping Mud busy and needed than I was about the baby. Christmas with two preschoolers and a new baby was hectic but fun. Barbara nursed well and slept soundly. Karen and David held her and observed and reported her every move. Mud clucked because I did not always retreat into the privacy of our bedroom for the intimate feeding process. We felt like a contented, complete family. "Third children are easy," I thought to myself.

The winter months that followed brought a TB scare. A neighbor and former babysitter died during tuberculosis lung surgery, and all of us (except Barbara who had never been in contact with her) were given skin tests. Karen's and David's turned out to be violently positive, and X rays showed that they had both weathered mild cases of TB. Karen was completely healed, but David's X rays still looked a bit doubtful and he needed to be watched for a while. The situation temporarily diverted my worries about Barbara.

Dr. Lloyd Hall took us through this time calmly and carefully. He had recently joined our local medical group, and our previous family doctor had moved to another town. We were fast becoming friends with the Halls and spending much time together. Spring came, the rain stopped, and all was well.

Edith Hall also had two small children and an infant, and we both began to suffer from cabin fever. We managed to accomplish marvels of accelerated housework and were often ready for "banana-box-outings" well before noon. Then we'd pack a simple lunch, extra panties, and diapers, and pile the tots in the car. The babies were stashed in banana boxes. These cardboard boxes make snug cribs and are easy to carry by the handholds in each end. We had an endless choice of favorite places where the children could run and play safely. With luck and good management our babies napped after lunch, and we mothers had a chance for adult conversation. What a happy set-up!

During that spring the first uncomfortable feelings began to surface in my consciousness. The Halls' banana box baby was a month and a half older than Barbara, but what a difference! Was it just because he was a boy? At home I reached for Gesell's book on child development and looked at the pictures. I did this often, each time more surreptitiously, as if I were afraid of being caught. What I read in the text and saw in the photos didn't make me feel better. Barbara seemed far behind the babies in the book, and although Karen and David had not been junior athletes at her age, I was certain that they had been much more active.

Al was of little help to me at this stage. I wanted to talk about my observations and anxieties. He growled at me everytime I touched the subject. "You must be getting old, dear! You never used to worry so when Karen and David were babies. Why don't you relax and enjoy her?" So I put Gesell back on the shelf. Way back! Like an addict I hid it behind other books and promised myself not to look at it for at least a month.

Karen was the first member of our family to echo my fears. I was changing Barbara's diaper one day, with Karen kneeling at the south end of the bassinet wielding the powder, when she asked, "Why doesn't our baby ever do anything, Mom?" I was still trying to think of an answer when she continued almost accusingly, "Keith rolled off the bed today when Edith changed him!" I can't remember what I said, but I know that her question registered as a milestone.

The next signal was given to me on a sunny afternoon later that summer. My parents had arrived to meet their newest grandchild. Barbara was eight months old, and my father was an observant physician. We were sitting in the garden when I heard the phone ring. "Here hold her a minute, please!" and I dumped Barbara into my father's lap before dashing for the house. When I returned, Papi was looking at the baby with a bemused look on his face. "You know, Lotte," he said as he gave her back to me, "she should have yelled when you handed her to me so abruptly." My ears heard his words, but my worried heart was not ready to cope with the essence of his message, so I filed away another incident in my cache of gnawing doubts.

By the time Barbara was a year old, I was finding it impossible to ignore those doubts. Why wouldn't she, why couldn't she get going? Madge Relyea, Mendocino County's first public health nurse, came to supper one night and looked at Barbara's backside suspiciously. Barbara had two creases below one buttock, which was normal, but only one on the other side, which, she said, might be an indication of a structural congenital hip condition. "This would certainly explain why she isn't crawling or walking. Perhaps we should make an appointment for her with Crippled Children's Services soon."

I took Gesell's book off the shelf one more time and found that the difference between our baby and little Keith Hall had become astronomical. At fourteen months Keith was a buster of a babe. His sturdy legs bowed slightly apart by Pampers, he toddled all over the place—around, over, and under seemingly insurmountable obstacles. He started to spend occasional overnights with us, and in the morning he'd lift himself onto a small chair in the kitchen, where he sat howling impatiently and pounding the table with his spoon until I managed to put a bowl of hot cereal in front of him.

Barbara, on the other hand, was patience personified. She rarely cried for her food, though she tackled it vigorously once it was served. She was able to roll from her tummy to her back but couldn't turn the other way, and she sat up only when we propped her up against a solid object. We had to childproof the house for Keith because everything went into his mouth, while Barbara sat surrounded by her toys and was just now trying to grasp objects with her hands.

I put away the old playpen as an unnecessary restraint. I knew in my heart of hearts that I would cheer her on the day that she started "getting into things."

The chickenpox siege during the next spring brought

matters to a head. All three of our children caught it—
Karen first, David next, and then Barbara. Each of them
waited their turn for the full twenty-one-day incubation
period, and I felt as if I had been "Nurse Nancy" forever.
One morning our family doctor dropped by for a house-
call. He dispensed pills and expert advice and then
settled down for a cup of coffee. "Aside from the chickenpox, Lloyd," I ventured wearily, "what do you think of
Barbara's overall development now?"

"Why don't you leave Lloyd alone," roared my husband. "Can't you let him have his coffee in peace?"

"Now wait a minute, Al," said Lloyd. "Perhaps this
would be a good time to talk about it. Barbara is fifteen
months old, and I think many a mother would have
rushed her child down to the University of California
Hospital long before this."

We talked. We made plans. We took steps. Of course I
was still afraid, but the fear was not quite as threatening
as before. I felt a little better because we were finally
doing something for Barbara.

The first stage of the odyssey was an appointment with
Dr. Peck, a pediatrician in Santa Rosa, one hundred and
ten miles from home. Barbara was seventeen months old
now. She was still not walking and quite heavy. I grate-
fully accepted Olga's offer to come along and help me. It
was a long, tiring trip. Dr. Peck asked endless questions
and seemed to be going over Barbara with a fine-toothed
comb. Then he referred her to a neurologist for further
tests and X rays of her hips, and of her head, which
appeared to him to be abnormally small. We had to spend
a night in a motel and return to his office in the morning.

"There is much that is normal about your little girl,"
he assured me. "Her hips and lower spine seem to be

okay, but there are a few things to be concerned about." He showed me the skull X rays, which had been essentially nonconclusive for whatever he was looking for. During the night I had remembered something about young Al, my husband's first-born son. While I knew that my own head and Al's were large, young Al had once jokingly referred to his pointed head, for which the U.S. Navy had found it difficult to find a small enough hat. Dr. Peck was interested in this bit of hereditary information, and eventually the worry about a possible diagnosis of microcephaly faded. "I would like to refer you to a specialist at the University of California Medical Center," he told me. He did not give me the definite diagnosis I had hoped for, but he was friendly, warm, and willing to answer my questions, and I had confidence in him.

Barbara's evaluation at the University of California Clinic took another two days. I had a hunch that it was going to be a siege, but I was not prepared for such a molten experience. In those days it took at least five hours to drive to San Francisco. Thank goodness Olga again offered to come along and help. Barbara's first appointment—for a psychometric test—was scheduled for nine in the morning, so we had to stay overnight again, and I prepared a crib-type bed for her in a hotel closet. We took along her stroller, for she was still not walking, and I knew that parking near the hospital would be difficult.

I had never experienced a public clinic. The impersonality of it appalled and intimidated me. As a doctor's daughter I had always had very personal medical attention. Here long lines of people waited in corridors or rested on hard wooden benches. There was no place to put down a small child for a nap and no lunchroom or handy vending machines. The memory of long noisy hall-ways and even longer waits between appointments is still uncomfortably clear. After the psychological test we were interviewed by a social worker who filled out endless forms. Half a dozen residents and interns poked and prodded Barbara at irregular intervals. They asked me questions but never volunteered an answer. I had no way of knowing if one of them was the specialist we had come to see, for they would come and disappear without bothering to introduce themselves.

Towards the end of the second afternoon, a nurse led us into a small examining room. She said that the professor would be coming to speak with us soon. Barbara looked grubby and felt cranky. She was thoroughly bored with the entire process and with the few toys that I had brought from home. She was chewing on a tongue depressor when the door opened and a middle-aged, slightly paunchy gentleman came in. "I'm Dr. Cohen," he said as he shook my hand and halfway propped himself against the examining table on which I had been sitting. He was followed by half a dozen men and women in white coats, who obviously weren't going to fit into the tiny room, so they stayed in the doorway. One or two of them looked faintly familiar. They were the pokers and prodders of yesterday and today. "So that's Barbara," Dr. Cohen said and waved to her from across the room. "Well, mother," he continued. "She will probably never make Phi Beta Kappa, but that will bother her a lot less than it will you."

Beyond that I remember very little. I was too tired and confused to ask many questions. Dr. Cohen had nice eyes and a warm smile, but he appeared hurried. He instructed me to check with a social worker on the way out. She would want to take my address so that we could make unspecified future plans. "Regards to Dr. Peck," he said as he left. "And let me see Barbara again in half a year."

I don't believe that the words "mental retardation" were spoken on that occasion. We returned to Dr. Peck's office in Santa Rosa a few weeks later to discuss the results of the University of California Clinic evaluation. Again it was summertime and the grandparents were visiting us, so my father volunteered to come along.

When we were all led into the doctor's office, the two physicians put their heads together, but Papi pulled out of the huddle, looked at me, and said: "No, no, doctor. You can tell Lotte, too. She's strong. She can handle this." Instinctively he appealed to my courage and thus buffered the news and the hurt of the diagnosis. Barbara did indeed have mental retardation.

5 *It Feels Like That Time Before*

THIS HURT WAS BAD. Hearing Barbara called retarded hurt like hell. Although we knew nothing about mental retardation, the concept had strong, even hopeless, overtones that had been indelibly connected with it by years of societal fear and prejudice. Our chubby, cuddly child was suddenly being relegated to a darkened future.

The pain conjured up devastating experiences that I had buried in the past. Now I was forced to look at them again. By replaying the film of my life, I could recall when I had felt good, and I also realized that earlier agonies had always disappeared gradually. I had to make sure that I would somehow be able to go on. It was a slow process. My busy life as a finicky housewife, mother of three, and occasional substitute teacher did not give me much time to sit and go into trancelike retreats.

How did I feel? It's hard to remember. Thoughts and feelings never stand still. Like the surf at the edge of the sand they advance and retreat, sometimes gently and at other times with stormy force. The shock and pain I now recall have been healed by the feelings of hope and optimism that have come from knowing Barbara and seeing her grow up. I do remember that I felt a little better after my doubts about Barbara's development had been replaced by a definite diagnosis, but the problem itself was there—huge and immovable as a rock.

Through three pregnancies I had taken it for granted that our children would all be healthy and bright. The concept "mental retardation" had never entered my head. The words shocked and frightened me. I felt sorry for myself, and I prayed as I had not done since those adolescent days in Hitler's Germany that I might wake up one morning and find that this was all a bad dream.

I am sure that I fit the prototype of the newly wounded mother during that summer of 1955. I must have been in the first of the three stages which professionals of the day assigned to the parents of children with disabilities.

First you feel guilty and wonder what you have done wrong to give birth to such a child—to shatter the dream of the perfect heir and the promise of immortality.

Next you exchange this period of sorrow and introspection for one of action, which is not necessarily purposeful or coordinated. It is, however, some activity outside of your own head and heart. This could be a "shopping trip" from one specialist to another in an attempt to exchange the initial diagnosis for something less hurtful. Some people manage to skip this stage and move directly towards one of purposeful activity, in which they try to find ways to help their child move towards a more hopeful future. The third stage often involves cooperation with other parents in trying to locate or establish educational programs, appropriate therapy, and the like.

I assume that these three stages of parental grief are still taught in many college classes. There are places in our country today—a lot of places, I hope—where the announcement, "Your baby has a problem," is coupled with a referral to other parents who have been there.

Talking with someone who has had a similar experience provides a tremendous buffer to the new parents' pain and shortens their grieving period.

I'm sure I took the long course. In the first of the three stages I wondered secretly if I might have done something wrong at some time during my pregnancy, but those thoughts dead-ended. I vaguely remembered a slip and a fall near the woodstove in our dining nook, but I had bounced lightly and hurt nothing. There had been a minor illness making its rounds during the early months of my pregnancy, which might have been German measles, but I had already had the disease, and my doctor said one can't catch it twice. My pregnancy had been smooth and uneventful. Nobody seemed to know of any genetic reason. Then why?

Uncontrollably my thoughts would then wander from the pregnancy to the actual birth process. Had there been a difference in the quality of care during Barbara's birth and that of Karen and David, and if so, what had it been?

Karen had been delivered by a general practitioner in Fairbanks, and my father had managed to throw his grandfatherly shadow all the way from New York to Alaska. Right from the start Papi took a dim view of my producing a first grandchild in the northern wilderness, and so when I wrote him that our Dr. Weston would be coming to New York for a medical conference, he went to great lengths to meet his young colleague and took him out for lunch to the finest French restaurant he could think of. I suspect that they talked about my pregnancy and care and that Dr. Weston felt extra responsible until the day of Karen's birth. I was proud and elated then, with the baby safely out and the feeling rapidly returning to my lower end, but Dr. Weston seemed to go on and on with the sewing of my episiotomy. "Just one more stitch," he insisted over my yowls that he was starting to hurt me. "We've got to do a good job here so Lotte's father will be pleased," he said to the nurse, as if he really believed that my father would inspect anything but the end product of the delivery!

With David's birth in New York I had the most loving and expert care a woman could expect. Dr. Langstadt was not only a friend of the family, but also an experienced obstetrician who had never lost a baby in fifty years of medical practice. He was doubly supportive because of Al's being overseas, and besides, he knew something that he would not let me know. (If he were alive today, I believe that he would level with pregnant women in such cases.) During one of my prenatal exams he prodded and poked my abdomen mightily. "Hey! Why are you being so rough today?" I asked him. He gave an excuse. Actually, he was trying to turn the baby into a head-down position in my uterus, but David did not cooperate and insisted on being a breech birth.

I labored from early morning until evening, and all during that long, hot June day Dr. Langstadt was close by, often holding my hand, and even during the tricky last stage of birth he supported me when I insisted that I did not want to have any anesthesia.

When I went into labor with my third child, I discovered that deliveries in small rural hospitals twenty-five years ago were a little more haphazard. Fort Bragg's doctors were overworked. Some of them lived miles out of town and could not come in for deliveries until the last minute. Because of the distances involved, they frequently had to cover for one another when babies made unscheduled appearances. The evening Barbara went into action, our regular physician was out of town, and there were two elderly nurses on the night shift. It was customary for one of them to take a nap in the linen room if all was calm. I lay in a regular bed in a six-bed ward and "labored" as efficiently and quietly as I could, all by myself. After all, I was an old pro with my third pregnancy and considered myself somewhat of a pioneer in the "Childbirth Without Pain" movement of Dr. Grantley Dick Read. I had read this British gynecologist's book and practiced his new method of exercises and relaxation in 1949 when I was expecting Karen. Both she and David were born while their mother was awake and aware.

With Barbara I went into heavy labor sometime during the early morning hours. My roommate, who was the proud mother of a day-old boy, had just asked the nurse for a bedpan when I needed to be rolled into the delivery room. That poor woman sat on the throne for about an hour. She claimed that she had a permanent ring on her bottom by the time the nurse came back to liberate her. We still joke about it when we run into each other in the grocery store and compare notes on our children.

It took the doctor awhile to drive into town, and I think I was holding back from those last almighty thrusts which might have pushed out the baby earlier. In those days we had no fetal monitors with which one could check on a baby's heartbeat during delivery. Perhaps Barbara did not get enough oxygen during that slow last stage of birth. We'll never know, but I have always wondered.

Such broodings, however, were clearly counterproductive. Dishes and dust cooties piled up and made me feel worse. I put my guilty thoughts and retroactive wonderings aside and discovered the healing qualities of movement and work.

In many ways nothing seemed to change in our daily doings after we came home with "The Diagnosis." We continued our orderly, busy lives. Karen was now in the first grade and seemed to fall into reading like a duck into water. David looked forward to kindergarten. Barbara was almost two. I remember it as my gray period.

We worked mightily. The printshop was an all-consuming effort for Al. He left for work right after breakfast, took a sack lunch, and did not return until time for dinner. I'd have the children all scrubbed and in their bathrobes—ready to tell him of their adventures and accomplishments of the day. Except for Barbara. She had started saying single words like "Mama" and "Dada" when she was a year and a half, but not much more speech had developed since then. She would be sitting propped up against the refrigerator, waving her arms ecstatically and welcoming her daddy with an enchanting smile. He gave her a full share of his attention and included her in the bedtime story and tucking-in ceremony with her own special piggy-back ride into bed.

On many evenings Al took a nap after dinner and returned to his shop for several more hours. He put in a full day on Saturdays and several hours of work on many a Sunday too. I began to watch anxiously for his return at supper time, for if he was loaded down with boxes, it meant hours of folding, collating, or putting stamps on business envelopes. The "women's handwork" of the printing trade, as it was then called, wasn't bad when we did it together, but it was deadly dull on lonesome evenings when Al had returned to his shop. We had no television then, so I listened to the radio or played reams of records and worried about Barbara.

She was certainly making progress all the time. Our

neighbors could see it and told me so. I entered each developmental milestone in her small blue health record: "First tooth at five months; sat unsupported at ten months; began to grab things with hands at twelve months." By the time we celebrated her second birthday and the Christmas of 1955, she had begun to crawl and was playing with her new peg toy. She was talented in other ways, too. She had learned to feed herself with a spoon and participated proudly in potty training.

When we went on an occasional family picnic or a hike with friends, Al patiently carried Barbara on his broad shoulders while other kids her age toddled around under their own steam.

With all of his great love and warmth and patience, Al could not yet face up squarely to his little girl's problems. Stubbornly he continued to quarrel with the dour predictions of the doctors, and I had a heck of a time to discuss her future with him. One evening I invited our friend Ed for supper. Ed is the father of the young man from whom Al took over the printshop. He taught printing and other industrial arts subjects at our high school, and the conversation that evening got around to education in general and to our youngest daughter's educational future in particular. I wondered what sort of practical courses a child like ours could take and asked Ed about the vocational offerings of Fort Bragg High School. Al argued angrily with me. Any child, given quality teaching by patient teachers could learn any academic subject, he maintained. He really believed that Barbara might be able to learn mathematics and physics if only we tried hard enough. At the end of the debate I felt defeated.

With most of our friends and neighbors we seldom talked about our worries. They knew of our trips to the city, and we made no bones about the diagnosis of mental retardation, but if they thought of Barbara as different, they did not tell us then. We included her in all our outings, and everyone seemed to accept her as one of the kids. The young couples with whom we spent time and exchanged baby-sitting services were tremendously helpful, especially Edith Hall, the wife of our family doctor. At the end of a baby-sitting afternoon I could relax over a cup of coffee and air my worries without getting blasted, and we'd compare notes on the children's interactions and the babies' bowel movements. Sometimes Edith would tell me about Barbara's newest accomplishment. She had held a toy or almost turned from her back to her stomach. In spite of the demands of our six small children, Edith managed to spend time on her very own mobility program for Barbara.

Our three grandparents were, of course, intensely concerned and involved. During the winter we wrote to them regularly. Summer brought Nana, Papi, and Mud to our house for several months. Interestingly enough, their attitudes towards Barbara and our family's problem differed sharply. My father's was naturally clinical. From time to time he would come up with a new thought or theory and ask me to check it out with our doctor. "Has Barbara had a thyroid test?" he wondered, and I reported back to him as soon as I found out. Overall though, he could find no fault with the doctors' diagnosis and recommendations. They had done a thorough, careful job and I am still impressed today when I look over their reports of twenty-five years ago.

My mother seemed to accept Barbara quite matter-of-factly. During her many years as a visiting grandma she became the official recorder of the children's growth and development, for she came loaded with film. Papi used to accuse her of "shooting from the hip," and often she did cut off a head or two, but there are many good photos in our albums. Nana intuitively understood that she could be as firm and as strict with Barbara as she had been with Karen and David, and once Barbara was able to get around on her own, she had no trouble taking care of her. After my father died and she moved into an apartment here in town, she willingly looked after Barbara whenever we asked her to, until her own health began to fail.

Al's mother, Grandma Mud, showed her love for her youngest grandchild in a different way. She never did seem to overcome her feelings of hurt and sorrow for us and for Barbara. Even years later, when she, too, had moved to an apartment here, she loved Barbara to a fault. We patiently tried to explain that we wanted her to treat Barbara like any other little girl. Barbara also had to learn limits. "Please don't let her have any candy when she visits you today!" we'd plead. "She's too chubby now and it'll ruin her teeth." Mud's invariable refrain would be, "Oh, let her—she enjoys it so!" with pity in her voice. Many years later, when Barbara had grown into a teenager, I overheard Mud say to an elderly friend: "Yes, isn't she pretty? Too bad she's so sick!" Inwardly I groaned about our failure to convince her that Barbara's slowness and special developmental needs called for a positive approach and that while she was slow in learning some things, she certainly was not sick.

During the early years of Barbara's life, Karen and David were the healing ingredients in our recovery process. We watched them move and grow apace, and they kept us all busy with Blue Birds, Cub Scouts, Sunday School, and Open House at the elementary school.

Regardless of how busy Al was, he took the time to take part in any and all gatherings that required the presence of parents. He was the one who loaded the stroller into the trunk of the car, packed Barbara onto his back, or bundled three sleepy children from car to bed after we had spent an evening visiting or square dancing. Karen and David took their little sister pretty much for granted during those early years. They were interested enough to report on her progress and applaud her efforts, but when she violated their territorial rights (all three shared one bedroom and and a large toy box), they protested loudly.

The first report from the University of California Clinic states that "the mother feels that the child is making constant improvement." I firmly believe that this was the key to Barbara's progress. We thought she would and so she did. Al especially continued to challenge her with high expectations, and—slowly but surely—she lived up to them and proved him right.

Luckily, I did not rush to the library to read everything and anything I could find, as I had done during David's TB scare. The card index renderings on mental retardation in a small town library of the fifties would have been sparse and depressing. There were no books then like Bob Perske's *New Hope for Parents of Persons Who Are Retarded*, which might have helped us work through our fears. Besides, a part of me—influenced by Al—was still hiding behind the thin veil of hope that Barbara's problem would turn out to be the kind of slow learning that one can remedy with extra tutoring. Perhaps Barbara's handicap would be like my brother Henry's slow start in school. I remembered how he had blossomed thanks to Nana's patient daily help with homework.

My gray period burst into furious red on the day a little

parcel arrived in the mail. At first I didn't even recognize the name of the sender. Then I remembered. She was a woman I had met while sitting on one of those brown wooden benches at the University of California Clinic several months before. She was sending me Dale Evans Rogers's book, *Angel Unaware,* with best wishes for our family. One look at the jacket blurb and I was indignant. How could it have been so obvious to her that our child had mental retardation? The Rogerses' baby had died. They had viewed her as a special gift from heaven and a very temporary visitor on earth. How could this woman put our robust, rosy-cheeked Barbara into the same bag with the Rogerses' slowly fading "angel"? But, she had made that connection, and that's what hurt!

It was both a bad shock and a good shock. For the first time I was able to see Barbara as others saw her. I could recognize the words "mental retardation" as the all-encompassing concept that it is to most people, which wipes out individual differences in their eyes and hopes in the hearts of parents. To the world out there, our child would be "different" and thus relegated to a segregated future. That was the red fighting flag.

Our hopes see-sawed along for the rest of that year, and we measured Barbara's smallest progress with pride. My thoughts were beginning to run far ahead. I wanted to plan and protect her twenty years into the future. Should we try putting her into a private nursery school? Would they let her into kindergarten? How about love and marriage? Al steadfastly maintained that she was outgrowing her problem, and now we realize that we were both right and that Barbara landed somewhere between his stubborn positive presumptions and my activist anxieties.

In the spring of 1956, when she was two years and four

months old, she started to walk. It happened at Edith and Lloyd Hall's house while I was out of town with David and Karen to keep an appointment with the orthopedist. We stopped at Al's shop on our way home. "Better go pick up Barbara right away," he said, unable to contain his excitement. "They have a surprise for you." The surprise was Barbara. Edith and Kris, their six-year-old, had let go of her hands and helped her reach this monumental milestone. She was actually walking alone. It was a funny-looking walk, but we thought it was beautiful. There she stood, straddle legged, both hands gripping the straps on her denim overalls for dear life, her tongue sticking out between her lips. The several steps she took towards us were wobbly, but she was proud as punch.

So Barbara was able to walk into the office of the University of California professor when we returned a year later. "Dr. Cohen would like you to bring your husband and Barbara's siblings if at all possible," the secretary had said when I phoned for an appointment. "Doctor likes to talk with the whole family."

It was a much more pleasant visit than the one the year before. Having the whole family together made it seem almost like an outing. Dr. Cohen's private office was warm and comfortable, and we hardly had to wait at all. Al and I went in first with Barbara, and Al was finally able to meet the doctor about whom I had spoken so much. Dr. Cohen examined Barbara briefly and noted her progress. Then Al and I had a chance to air our different expectations.

"No!" Dr. Cohen said honestly. "This will *not* go away. She will not outgrow the problem, but in your good family you can expect to see her develop. Let me see her again later, and now I would also like to talk with Karen and David."

He was excellent with our two older children, now five and seven years old. The crux of his message was, "Help your small sister with all the things that you know how to do, but don't help her too much. Let her try. Don't do things for her!"

On that day he cut them in as partners on our family team, and we began to learn from each other—all five of us.

6 Must You Do It, Mother?

SOON AFTER WORLD WAR II parents of children with developmental special needs erupted into action like spontaneous combustion. It happened on different continents and in many different countries. These stubborn, belligerent, constructive efforts grew from parents' mutual concern about their children into a force for change that we proudly call the parent movement.

The parent movement had come to Fort Bragg early in the fifties, before Barbara was born. Several women with mixed backgrounds in teaching, occupational therapy, social work, and homemaking observed parents with handicapped children in the stores and on the steets. In a small town one notices such things. What happened to such children in our town? "Not much" was the answer, and a few phone calls and a couple of cups of coffee later, the nucleus of an organization and the beginnings of a program came into being.

The group was able to hire a woman to sit with the children three mornings a week in a local church for fifty cents an hour. "We really intended this service as nothing more than relief for the parents," Josephine Wheeler, the founding president, told me recently. "We certainly didn't think that they were capable of learning." The program had to be discontinued when the salaried person moved away, but under Jo's leadership the Parents and Friends of Retarded Children, Inc., was duly incorporated in 1955 and became one of the first such parent organizations in the state of California.

Al and I weren't ready for this yet. As a matter of fact, we hardly knew the group existed. I vaguely remember reading small notices about their meetings in the weekly *Advocate*, but the thought of going to a meeting didn't occur to me. And those members who knew me well refrained from urging me to join them. One did not easily inflict such a painful invitation on a friend.

The first task of the early parent associations was to identify the developmental special needs of their children. They needed to describe what was wrong before they could apply pressure for necessary programs and services.

Now we know that all children have strong and weak suits. We can often measure and plot the high and low points on a developmental profile and then build bridges to strengthen the overall functioning of every child. We are usually able to zero in on each person's developmental special need without hanging a stigmatizing, permanent label around his or her neck.

I couldn't have explained any of this back in 1956. Our family acted on hunches. Barbara's strong suits had to do with hunger and elimination. She fed herself by hand or by spoon at about the same time and with the same messy eagerness of other children her age. Toilet training also proceeded on schedule. Because we cheered successes and didn't make a big deal about messes, she learned these skills proudly and well. Her speech and gross motor coordination, however, were noticeably slow. Were she a

71

toddler today, she could benefit tremendously from extra help in these areas.

I used to pray that Barbara would learn to talk. Our family is an articulate bunch, and the prospect of establishing a communicating relationship without speech seemed overwhelmingly difficult. Barbara's little blue medical record book states that she said "Mama" and "Dada" when she was nineteen months old and that she was able to play "patty cake" about the same time. The fact that she was able to recognize members of our family and others who were close friends was evident from the gleeful expression on her face and that overall body wiggle which is a language in itself.

We listened patiently to Barbara's every monosyllable. "Guess what Barbara said today!" became standard reporting procedure, and one day she really surprised us. She was walking by then, so she must have been about two and a half years old. She picked up a penny from the floor in the grocery store and brought it to me. "Mummy, money!" she said, clearly differentiating between the two middle consonants. This was more than a person's name or an object word repeated. She had made a statement that expressed a concept, and this delighted us. We aren't a money-oriented family, so we were amazed to discover our youngest daughter's early financial bent. Her pronouncement was also encouraging because we knew that if she could say two words that reached outside of her immediate family constellation, she would learn other concepts in time.

So we bumbled along with our stimulation program, unplanned and disorganized as it was. When Karen and David were little, we had seldom allowed them to stay up late. We believed in regular bedtime hours and plenty of sleep, but Barbara seemed to be brighter when her routine was changed. She was animated instead of crabby on the morning after. So the stroller was put into the back of the car more and more often, as PTA potlucks, school recitals, and friendly picnics required our presence.

It was a good thing that Barbara liked riding in cars, for to this day a steady stomach, strong spine, and patient backside are prerequisites for getting from Fort Bragg to almost anywhere else. Karen had been a wiggleworm from the beginning. When she was a baby, she refused to sit in carseats and crawled all over her exasperated grandma, while I drove my father's car around New York. Back home in Mendocino County, she'd start to squirm five miles down the road and ask, "When do we get to San Francisco? How much longer is it?" David was the exact opposite. As long as the wheels were turning, he was happy and wide-eyed. I hoped that this wasn't a male characteristic and it was not. Barbara also rode happily wherever we took her. In fact, both Karen and I required many more service station stops than she did.

Other aspects of family outings, however, weren't necessarily smooth and easy. Barbara used to cry out in fear at the sudden dimming of lights in an auditorium or theater, and when she met a friend downtown who was a favorite, she expressed her delight in strange ways. She pummeled the person with her fists, screeched, and threw herself on the ground. We didn't understand why she did this. Was the reason that the words of joy and recognition would not come out? At any rate, people now tell us that they wondered if she would ever learn to behave like other children.

Once a friendly fireman in San Francisco showed our children the big red engine. As a special treat he rang the bell for them. The sound reverberated in the tiny station house. Barbara screamed in terror and we had to calm her and thank him at the same time. But gradually she got used to most of the strange sights and sounds of her environment and learned to act more appropriately. Her greatest early triumph occurred during a Saturday children's matinee at the local movie theater.

She won the drawing for the big prize—a bicycle. Karen and David reported how well she handled the situation. They called her name and asked her to come up on stage to accept the prize. She climbed the steps slowly.

"Is your name Barbara Moise?" asked the manager.

She nodded and beamed.

"Would you like to say something?"

"Thank you," she said clearly, and everyone applauded.

She never learned to ride that bike, but it remained in her possession for years. She took great pride in owning it, and from time to time she wheeled it out of the shed and pushed it around the house. Al spent many hours trying to teach her how to ride, but she didn't seem to have the balance and coordination for the rough and bumpy ground around our house.

When Barbara mentions that bike today, I realize how much was missing in her early gross motor development program. We knew that our baby was lying on her back far too long and that she was sitting still too patiently. But it took endless hours to hold her in a standing position or to encourage her to take a step. There didn't seem to be enough hours in the day, and I probably wasn't patient enough. I tended to be compulsive about doing housework first, whereas Edith, at whose house Barbara had taken those first momentous solo steps, could ignore messes and work with Barbara in spite of them.

The public health doctor, to whom we took all our children for required shots and immunizations, told us that Barbara had flat feet. "Congenital flat feet" the orthopedist in a distant town added. "Better keep her in high top boots with arches and steel shafts," he said, but that was the extent of his advice. Nobody quite realized how important it would be for her future mobility to strengthen specific muscles and to encourage balance and coordination. The skills and support of a physiotherapist or recreation therapist would have helped us immensely in structuring our program for Barbara's motor development.

It saddens me now when I look at our awkward, uncoordinated and often fearful daughter and think of the skills she might have learned. She might have learned to ride that bike, to climb up and down steep places, and to get on and off escalators. There is little doubt in my mind that we could have taught her to bridge more of the gaps in her coordination, because she loosens up and looks ecstatically happy when she dances and in the water she relaxes and swims well.

Later on, when I became a special education teacher, I blundered into physical activities for our students as the need for them crossed my inexperienced mind. The schoolhouse was poorly insulated and icy cold on winter mornings, so it made sense to warm up with exercises. Music seemed to support movement, so we danced. A heated pool was available, so we taught swimming. It all just happened, and it happened for the best.

Barbara now asks me occasionally why she cannot drive a car. We talk about it, and I try to help her face the reality of her physical limitations. I remind her of her aunt who never learned to ride a bike or drive a car and our neighbor who can't swim. It is sad for her and for us, but it is as real

75

as the physical condition that puts others into wheel-chairs. In hope of consoling her, I tell Barbara about my awkward attempts at skating and skiing when I was younger and how I decided to give up these particular activities. Still, the confession of my own failures is small consolation in our mobile, motorized world, and we find it difficult to strike a fine balance between encouraging her to try and discouraging unrealistic expectations.

Our early stimulation program for our little girl continued to be haphazard as we worked with her, four ways towards the middle. I taught her to recognize colors from a Hudson's Bay blanket. Every morning when she helped me make our double bed, we played games with the bright red, green, black, and yellow stripes on the blanket. "Show me the red! Is this green?" I would say, as I pointed to the wrong color over and over, until she knew and was able to identify and say these color words.

Phonograph records contributed greatly to the noise level of our house, and they became a valued teaching device. When the children were little, Al would wake us all up with his favorite startlers—bagpipes, drumbeats, and jazz. Later, Al and I were drowned out by our children's even noisier rock and country and western discs. Barbara loved music and rhythm. Singing along seemed to help new words come out. She surprised us in being smarter than her sister Karen in catching onto the workings of automatic record players. She handled them intelligently and carefully. Karen instinctively capitalized on this situation to build up Barbara's self-confidence. "Come here a minute, Barb! I can't start this thing," she would say, and Barbara would hurry over and make it play. Here was another puzzle in the unevenness of Barbara's development: if she could do this, why not something else?

Our favorite game at bedtime became "Hide the Thimble." It was Al's idea that it might sharpen Barbara's powers of observation and perception. She had had a slight problem with her eyes not tracking together when she was a baby, but this had corrected itself. Now it was more a problem of seeing what was right in front of her nose. So we hid the thimble all over our house, and Karen and David eagerly steered her in the right direction as she toddled from room to room in her bathrobe. "You're cold, Barb, icy cold. Now you're getting warmer. Hot! Hot! You *found* it!" And in the process she learned about up and down, in front of and behind of, and under and over—all essential concepts that other children learn without prompting.

During these first five years of Barbara's life, we were still hoping that the public schools would provide whatever special education programs she would need. In the meantime, though, it seemed like a good idea to give her extra help to get ready for school. Karen and David had been busy enough without nursery school, but Barbara needed more stimulation than we could give her at home. When she was four, we enrolled her in a private nursery school along with three little neighbor girls, and it felt comfortably "normal" to me to be taking turns in the carpool.

It was through PTA work that I first recognized the efforts of our small local group of parents of children with developmental special needs. I attended a district meeting at which the featured speaker was the president of the California PTA. She was a wise and wonderful woman, who spoke eloquently of special education programs for children who were mentally retarded. She told us about certain new sections of the 1956 state of California education code which mandated that school districts of a certain size provide classes for the educably mentally retarded.

As the questions from the audience bounced back and forth over my head, I heard definitions of "educable" versus "trainable" mentally retarded, based on specific IQ points and cut-offs. When they weren't talking about these children as "educable" or "trainable," they seemed to be referring to them as "Point I" or "Point II." All of this sounded confusingly like a new language, but I soon found out that Points I and II were the tail ends of four-digit numbers designating sections of the state education code. For many years California youngsters with special developmental needs were labeled as Point I or Point II.

I had driven to the meeting with a group of PTA buddies, and as we moved through the buffet lunch line, I found myself talking to a woman whom I had never met before. She had driven over from Fort Bragg with her teenaged daughter. The girl was strangely quiet as her mother talked about her anxiously. It seemed that nothing was happening for her child in our school district in spite of the state mandates. Helen had attended regular classes when she was a little girl, but she had withdrawn into silence and was currently excluded from public school. Her mother had recently joined a local group of other parents who had retarded children in the hope that something could be done for her.

Sometime after this encounter, I attended a meeting of this group, Parents and Friends of Retarded Chidren, for the first time. They met in the basement of the junior high school near the boiler room. I felt uncomfortable about joining their shoestring operation in such a nonprestigious place, and I was far from ready to meet the challenge of being part of a pioneering movement. I simply wanted to find out more about our Barbara's chances for a school program.

Several older women in the group stood out from the rest. Mary Wilbur was a robust woman who had long ago raised her own family. She was presently fostering two children at her home near Fort Bragg. One of her little girls was on leave from our area's state hospital. Penny had no speech. She was a tiny, dwarflike creature who had to use her entire body to express anything she wanted to say. Her foster mother, though, had lots to say and energy to burn. Mary and I co-organized outings and picnics for our families that summer, and while we herded children and swapped recipes, she somehow helped me face certain unpleasant realities about our nonexistent service system. She not only complained loud and clear about the uncooperative attitude of Penny's social worker, but she also stood her ground on behalf of the child. That lady knew the ropes and gave me ideas.

Imbie Wirtnen was a retired teacher who was slightly handicapped herself by a limp due to a congenital hip condition. A pretty, gentle woman, she had the gift of diffusing anxiety with a twinkle and an anecdote. Even though Imbie was unmarried and childless, her motherly warmth embraced persons of all ages. Her neat house contained a toybox full of surprises, which attracted neighbor children by the dozen. Barbara loved to visit her, and we went often for advice and moral support. When the parent association first organized a part-time childcare service, she had been a faithful and effective volunteer teacher. She was still in there pitching when I first joined the group.

The third member of the troika was Ellen Taylor,

another retired teacher. For years she had taught a mixed bag of children in a small logging camp schoolhouse. Ellen was one of a breed of pioneer women that is now almost extinct, and she had practiced her profession undaunted by distance, weather, or individual differences.

One mother in the association—our historian—regularly reminded us of the way in which she had first received the diagnosis of her daughter's condition. Many years later the memory was still so painful that she often repeated this story. She had taken her pretty baby to a large teaching hospital to find out what caused her to be so slow. "A young resident put her back into my lap," she told us. "He almost threw her. And he hardly looked at me. And then he said, 'Sorry, Ma'am, but I think you should place her in a state hospital right away. She'll never be more than a vegetable.' Then he left."

She and her husband and their baby moved to our small town soon afterwards. She remembers the warm concern of strangers whom she met on the street and in stores, but it was frequently and bluntly expressed in a similar manner. "You're not going to keep her at home? There must be places for children like this!" But she steadfastly believed that there would be a place for her little girl close to home, and when I met her, she was patiently and efficiently working towards this goal as treasurer of the association.

I, too, began to feel involved with their fears and frustrations. Their hopes and aspirations for their children became my own. I came to the realization that I had to narrow my efforts from the PTA, with its goal of improving the quality of education for all children, to the more specialized and urgent needs of Barbara, which was the business of the Parents and Friends of Retarded Children.

Soon after I joined the association —sometime in 1957 or 1958—we received a couple of shocks in short order. We were now aware of the legislation which mandated special classes for children with mental retardation. Because I was a substitute teacher and knew the superintendent of schools, I was sent forth to tackle him on the matter of the new mandate. We liked each other, and we had campaigned together on the same side of the political fence.

"How about a special class for those of our children who fit the Point I category?" I asked him.

"I want to be frank with you, Lotte," he said thoughtfully, leaning back in his chair. "The way I feel about retarded children is that if they can maintain themselves in the regular classroom—fine and dandy. If not they should be in an institution."

To leave no room for doubt, he added, "No. Our district does not foresee starting a Point I class in the near future." And that was that.

His refusal to cooperate did not propel us into instant action. We were still afraid. About that time I met a man who was president of a local parent association in a small town east of the Sierras. He was organizing a lawsuit against his school district for noncompliance with the new mandate. "I think you're making a mistake," I told him. "In our association we believe in gentle persuasion." He spoke forcefully of his son's *right* to an education, and I was appalled by his militance. "My husband owns a small business, and besides, he's president of the Chamber of Commerce. We simply can't afford to be rebels and radicals!" Yes, we were still timid and afraid.

Something more was needed for us to stand up and take action. It happened in the office of the elementary school principal, when I took Barbara to an appointment with the school psychologist. We still hoped that she might be able to attend regular kindergarten. "Perhaps they will be able to hold her over for a second year," her nursery school teacher had suggested. She was a retired teacher and had heard of such cases. Another straw of hope! If Barbara could spend two years in kindergarten she'd be almost eight, and eight was the suggested starting age for special classes, Surely by then they would have one.

Barbara was wiggly and vague as I watched her "play games" with the psychologist. They permitted me to be in the room with them, since he was a total stranger to her. Having given intelligence tests myself, I could tell that she was doing miserably. The verdict was "No! Barbara is not nearly mature enough for kindergarten." And then the ultimate misery. "Hasn't anybody ever told you that she is Point II?"

It was then that I began to toy with the idea of getting a special education credential and trying to teach a class myself. On one hand it was a terrifying thought to attempt this outside of the public school system, but we were beginning to hear and read about others who were starting private schools and managing on their own. I conferred within my own family and with association members. When I mentioned my idea to Dr. Cohen, he asked, "Must you do it, Mother? Isn't there anyone else who could do it?" In his wisdom he foresaw the enormous energy such a venture would take, and he was probably considering how it might affect Karen and David.

An education professor from San Francisco State College was much more encouraging. Dr. George McCabe had taught an evening extension course on counseling and guidance in Fort Bragg, one rainy winter when Barbara was still a toddler. He had to stay overnight, and on several occasions those of us who took his course met informally after class for coffee and further talk. Thus Dr. McCabe knew of our problems, and I felt free to ask his advice about returning to school. I had a valid California secondary school credential and had just completed a couple of extension courses for an elementary credential. What else would I need? How much time would be required away from home? How much would it cost? What did he think of a mother teaching her own child?

In a long, thoughtful letter he replied, "Why not, Lotte? Barbara is lucky that you have the kind of background which will make it relatively easy for you to get the credential—and we'll help all we can at this end." He introduced me to Professor Jerome Rothstein, who gave me further information. It would take twenty-four additional credits for a special credential, but I did not need to take them all at once. A six-week summer session workshop, with philosophy, methods, curriculum, crafts, and classroom observation all rolled into one, would give me a special credential on postponement of requirements, and I could take the rest in dribs and drabs later.

Dr. Rothstein suggested that I apply for a fellowship from the Crown Zellerbach Foundation, and when I received it, Al and I knew that we'd be able to pay our babysitters for the summer as well as my room and board in San Francisco. Our parent group pledged their full support. With my credential I could be the qualified teacher, and as soon as we felt ready, we would begin a class.

Only one good friend had doubts about my venture and the honesty to voice them to me. "Why do you want to put so much energy into working with the retarded, when you have so much to offer normal children?"

And what about Karen and David? How would they survive six precious summer vacation weeks with only a weekend mother? Al and I decided to call a family conference. We explained that Sylvia and Eileen would be their babysitters. Though these women probably couldn't organize many beach trips and picnics, since neither of them knew how to drive, they would be good cooks and storytellers. I'd come home every Friday evening and stay until Sunday night. This would give me time to write up the week's menu, shop for food, and regroup the forces. "What do you think, children?" They thought. Karen spoke first. "Okay, Mom, if it's going to help Barbara get a class, okay." David nodded in agreement. We were on our way.

7 Teacher Goes to School

WE WERE UNAWARE OF IT THEN, but our family was embarking on a new way of life that summer of 1959.

Gone forever was my resolve that I would not work full time until we had raised our children. I had to leave home for parts of the next four summers to complete the special education credential. For the next ten years I worked full time while trying to love, please, and care for one husband, three children, and an assorted number of dogs, cats, lambs, a horse, and a duck.

Al was still putting in endless evening and weekend hours to build his printing business. David and Karen took part in Sunday school, Blue Birds, and Cub Scouts in addition to stretching their minds with books and testing their muscles with stilts, bikes, horses, hikes, and swimming. As a family, we celebrated every conceivable holiday on the calendar, and we all brought home our friends for fun and respite.

From time to time the children complained. "We never go anywhere," David wailed. "Nancy's parents took her camping," Karen informed us. "Dad works all the time—and now you, too, Mom!" Later, when they were able to look back at their childhood from the ripe old age of twenty or so, they gave Al and me passing grades as parents. True, David has never forgiven us for selling the vintage Rolls Royce without consulting him. And more than once Karen accused me of being neat and clean to the point of anal compulsion because I insisted that she tidy up her messy room. "But we always knew you were there," they both said. Somehow we must have managed to make up for the quick pace of our lives by the quality and intensity of our family interactions.

We survived the separation of my first summer away. In fact, it turned out to be a launching pad for us all. I learned to overcome my fear of the arts and crafts portion of the course. I knew well why I was so afraid of it. A grouchy bear of a first grade teacher in Germany had spoiled it for me for life, or so I thought. As the youngest student in her class, my fingers were clumsier than those of the others—and she had rubbed it in. Whether it was sewing on a button, crocheting a potholder, or drawing a vase, she had made me feel ashamed of the results. Years later, I felt just as inept. My friend Virginia Robertson gave me the push I needed. "Heavens, Lotte," she burst out, "if a kindergartner can learn to do those things, you can, too!" So, to my surprise, I discovered that I wasn't all thumbs after all. When I began to turn out creditable cutting, pasting, finger painting, and clay projects, my family's appreciation was touching. I found out how important it is, especially after experiencing failure, to receive praise and to be reinforced for small successes. Al hung my school painting in the bathroom to cover a hole in the paneling. Karen argued with David over who could put my blue cardboard wastebasket in their room. I was pleased and proud.

Al and the children also learned much that summer. On weekends I poured out descriptions of our class trips and observations, and I told them all about current theories, methods, and nomenclatures. Then the language of special education began to cause us anxiety. Sometime earlier we had jointly decided that Barbara should never have to hear the big, bad words "mental retardation." Instinctively, we shrank from wounding her with that term, but to spell out m-e-n-t-a-l r-e-t-a-r-d-a-t-i-o-n at the suppertable was obviously awkward, even for Papa the Printer and superspeller.

At the time it was clearly necessary to describe and define our children's special needs precisely. That's the only way we were able to get anywhere with the legislators and educators whom we were belaboring for programs. "But," we would add whenever we described the special conditions of mental retardation, "our children are more like other children than they are different." We believed it and were prepared to prove it by talking of our sons' and daughters' warmth and affection, their loyalty and love, their recognition of old friends and familiar tunes, and the practical skills they were learning from pioneer programs. We wanted it clearly understood that their problem of mental retardation was secondary to their humanness.

Each Friday evening after I drove home from San Francisco State after five days of intensive bombardment with mental retardation theory and five introspective hours alone on the road, I was struck anew with Barbara's solid membership status in our family. She laughed and cried, she hugged and hit, she smiled and pouted. Above all, she was our child, our youngest child, and we loved her.

In spite of all this, the trend of bandying labels about infected our family. So much of our time and energy went into thoughts about Barbara that we seemed unable to shield her from the words. Many, many years later she shamed us with her own protest. We were talking about one of her "retarded" classmates. "I *hate* that word!" she said.

I shall never forget one summer day in 1959. Our class went to visit a large state hospital, which at the time housed more than four thousand mentally retarded persons. An impressive array of administrators, physicians, psychologists, and top level ward personnel faced the students from behind a long table on the platform in the auditorium.

"Doctor so-and-so will now present the first patient. This is a thirty-three-year-old white, mongoloid female. . . ." droned the voice, as a woman slowly approached the center of the platform. "Now, Mary, will you tell me, . . ." the doctor continued in a kindly, but condescending tone, concluding with "Thank you, Mary," before he went on to the next case. The "patients" looked content enough. No doubt they were glad to be excused from work or to get away from the routine of ward living. We took copious notes and asked questions of the authorities lined up before us. There were to be no visits to the wards.

By chance one of the psychologists on the platform turned out to be someone I knew. She suggested that we skip lunch so that she could give me a guided tour. I eagerly took her up on the offer. My impressions of that tour have since become blurry, except for two of them.

I remember the outdoor play area of a "cottage" which housed crowds of young men who appeared to have no major disabilities. The entire area was enclosed with a wire fence—the tops as well as the sides—giving it the appearance of a bird cage in a zoo. Symbolically, this eliminated all possibility of flight!

And I remembered well into weeks of restless sleep the "cottage" where seventy little girls lived. All very much like our six-year-old Barbara at home. All trying to touch as they crowded and pushed and stumbled around me, vying for a hug or a word. All calling me "Mama" in their yearning for affection.

I saw our child, lovingly tucked into bed by her parents, surrounded by stuffed animals and crowded by favorite dolls. On that day I knew with overwhelming certainty that we were lucky to be able to keep Barbara at home— and that she would grow and develop in our family rather than wither in a warehouse. I now had commitment, a direction, and a cause. This was the impetus I needed to sustain my efforts and charge my energies for the years to come. I was working—and would continue to work—for decent dignified community living for my child and for all other children who happened to have developmental problems.

There were, of course, other learnings that took place that summer, and for better or for worse I soaked them all up. We were well indoctrinated in the existing knowledge of the day, which put mentally retarded students into small compartments for the convenience of school administrators. Schools received average daily attendance moneys based on these classifications, and classes were organized accordingly.

We drew dividing lines hard and fast. Educable mentally retarded children were those with IQs of fifty to seventy. They were considered capable of reading on an elementary level and might become economically and socially independent. Those with the label "trainable" were supposed to have IQs between thirty-five and fifty, and would, we were told, always require a protected environment. Work, marriage, and voting would not be for them. Classes for educable students were often located on a regular school campus. Those for trainable children were placed off by themselves in basements, barns, or little houses where the students were isolated, protected, and treated like the children they were supposed to be.

We were told that one always correlates chronological age with mental age. Joe Blow, at seventeen years of age, weighing one hundred and eighty-five pounds, is still a child if his IQ places him at the mental age of a five-year-old. Nobody told us that an IQ score is nothing more than a way of expressing the results of a particular test administered by a particular person and taken by an individual on a particular day.

Though I was beginning to feel some discomfort at this absolute IQ information, I was not yet able to connect it with our observations of Barbara. That came later. We were too close to the problem and needed time and distance. It was a bit like tennis. We learn our own mistakes of racket handling and body position by watching someone else or from the once-removed reflection of ourselves on a movie screen or video tape. In the meantime I came close to being entrapped by the IQ myth of the fifties.

Earlier, those in the professional community—special educators and psychologists—had designated three broad catagories of "mental deficiency" securely tied to IQ scores: "idiot" for those scoring below IQ 25, "imbeciles" from 25 to 50, and "morons" from 50 to 70 or 75. By the time I returned to college in 1959, these terms had been shifted from "idiot" to "severe," "imbecile" to "moderate," and "moron" to "mild." We thought we were being so progressive in making this change, and yet we were still putting children and adults into rigid, inflexible boxes, which kept them from any outward and upward movement.

In one respect the new nomenclature was even more restrictive than the old. Not only were people boxed in by the concept, "Once retarded, always retarded," now some of them were further constricted by being classified as "Once trainable, never educable." Such persons were placed on a narrow, irreversible conveyor belt which dead-ended in repetitive, nonproductive learning and precluded hope for further growth.

It was not until ten years later that educators would come to understand that many so-called trainable students functioned quite well outside of these IQ cubbyholes in their families, neighborhoods, and yes, on their jobs. With that we became aware of a factor above and beyond that of IQ and the ratio of chronological to mental age. We discovered the importance of "social adaptation," which helped to bring about open-ended programming.

I learned other interesting goodies that summer, many of which I later unlearned as I worked with Barbara and her classmates:

> Trainable retarded children have little concept of history or geography. Limit their lessons to the here and now.
> Trainables are less aware of their handicap than educables.
> They have a short attention span.
> Their memory is poor.
> They cannot handle abstractions, draw conclusions, or use judgment.

"Cannot, cannot, cannot" was always accompanied by the magical IQ cut-off to strengthen the artificial intellectual compartments into which we were placing these children in our well-intentioned professional wisdom.

My earlier professional preparation had certainly readied me for accepting these academic truisms. At Teachers College of Columbia University during the early forties, I had learned to give intelligence tests. They were used to assess normally bright youngsters and mastery of their administration was required for the counseling and guidance major. I owned a Stanford-Binet IQ testing kit, which I was sorely tempted to use. It would have been fun to see how bright Karen and David really were and to check on those test results of Barbara's. I knew, however, that the results of such tests, when given by a parent, would probably not be accurate. Because I might fudge with the interpretation of certain answers, I resisted temptation.

Both Al and I had been conditioned to think that smart is better than stupid and that an educated person is worth more than one who is ignorant. Both of our families valued professional education and respected white collar accomplishments. How did we escape total entrapment?

My own escape was partly due to my younger brother. During our childhood Henry was clearly less of a student than I. Music and trains were his overwhelming loves, and he just did not concentrate on academic subjects. Even though Nana coached him day after day, he never managed to get the easy A grades in school that I did. My father despaired of his ever making it into college and almost shamefully began to think of a trade school for his son. In Germany this was quite a comedown for a doctor. When we arrived in New York, Henry's studies did not improve. Although he graduated from high school and made it into a city college, his grades were a disaster. He barely squeezed through freshman English and got a D- in a science survey course after taking it three times.

Meanwhile, the psychology courses I was taking helped me learn more about the nature of intelligence. For the first time it hit me that Henry might be learning at a different rate of speed and in a different way. He might even prefer a kind of work which was not college based. I went to bat for him with Papi. "Why not let him take some business courses if he wants to?" I asked. World War II soon put an end to our family debate. It also matured the boy into a man who knew in what direction he wanted to go.

When Henry returned to college on the G.I. Bill of Rights, he majored in economics and maintained an A+ average. He zipped through four years of college work in two and half years and then went straight to graduate school for a master's degree.

Then there is Al. With the exception of a couple of Navy communications courses, he never went to college. He has worked hard with his hands most of his life, and he is without a doubt the ablest, warmest, and most sensitive man I have ever known.

And yet I almost swallowed the IQ myth. Although I had never thought of Al's or my own abilities in terms of an intelligence quotient, although I had steadfastly resisted the temptation of testing our children with that Stanford-Binet kit, I was vulnerable. In spite of the fact that I could see Barbara making slow but steady progress, I felt let down if one of her test scores was a few points lower than the time before. A slight increase raised wild hopes. Why? It was the pressure of knowing that our child was being asked to qualify for school programs which should have been rightfully hers. She had to be ready for school instead of the schools being ready for her.

Unfortunately, we have still not come out from under the shadow of the IQ myth. A short time ago, Barbara had to take a psychological test in order to qualify for Social Security benefits under her father's account. I had a chance to read the standard one-page assessment prepared by the certified psychologist who saw Barbara for a brief period of time. The IQ figure didn't startle me. It seemed to be approximately the same as I had remembered it from years ago. It was the rest of the report that appalled me. The man who tested Barbara had no way of knowing what she could do in terms of everyday living skills, and yet he called her severely retarded and added a few sentences about the areas in which he considered her incompetent. The report is so totally impersonal that the writer seems unaware of the young woman Barbara has become. Once again, the label has obscured the person.

8 *Paul Bunyan School*

WE DID NOT START "OUR SCHOOL" for another year. When I returned home from summer school, I was still unsure about whether I really wanted to become a working mother or not. I also had serious doubts about my teaching skills. The demonstration class which we had observed as students during the summer session seemed so difficult that I thought I could never teach a group like it.

For the summer the special education department had gathered together a group of children from a dozen school districts in San Francisco. They were strangers to each other, and the teacher had no previous experience with them. She worked alone since we students sat silently on the sidelines, and she did not have a teacher's aide. Her students' problems were varied. Some seemed extremely withdrawn while others acted out. One had uncontrolled seizures. We watched with awe as Marvel Glynn pulled this group of children together. I didn't feel ready or able to tackle a comparable task.

I happened to meet her again after she retired and opened a bookstore in Mendocino. I told her how her skillful teaching of that summer class had weakened rather than strengthened my own resolve. She laughed and said, "I almost didn't make it myself that summer!

D'you know I lost twelve pounds in those six weeks?" But neither she nor any of the other faculty members had let on. They did a masterful job of letting us think that this was a breeze.

Back home, I met one of our county's first special education teachers, who invited me to visit her class. It was a curvy drive of an hour and a half to Calpella, but I needed this opportunity to sample instruction methods for myself.

Typically, Mrs. Jamison and her students were housed off by themselves in a two-room country schoolhouse. The boys' and girls' restrooms were converted outhouses joined to the building by a slim covered walkway which barely protected against the rain. Mrs. Jamison put me to work as soon as she had introduced me. "Boys and girls, this is Mrs. Moise from Fort Bragg. She is a teacher, too, and is interested in what we are doing." I headed for the safety of a chair in the corner, but I barely got there before she said, "Ruth is doing a problem with clocks. Perhaps you can help her. Here, take this chair!"

Before the first day was over, I felt more confident. Mrs. Jamison was not only an excellent teacher, but a superb teachers' teacher as well. She made me a working partner and had a gift of explaining in few words what she was doing and why. This kind of teaching really felt no different than what I was accustomed to doing in the classroom. I spent many more days with her, and within a few months I was able to announce cheerfully at a parents' meeting, "Let's start our class in the fall."

It couldn't have happened without allies, of course. I met the chief one in a line of mothers waiting on brown wooden benches on a spring day in 1960. We were gathered in Fort Bragg's Veterans' Memorial Hall to be seen by a visiting team of doctors and psychologists from the nearest state hospital. It was a fearfully familiar room to many of the children, who had had their baby shots and childhood check-ups from the public health doctor there. Barbara was leery and restless. I was relatively calm, for I expected no new shocks from this encounter, but the young mother next to me was anxious and apprehensive. She introduced herself to me as Dodie Scott. She and her husband and son had recently moved to Fort Bragg from out of state. We talked about our children.

"Jeff has a heart murmur," she confided. "It's because he's mongoloid, but where we lived before, the doctor told me he might outgrow it. As a matter of fact, they never said anything to us when Jeff was born. We found out when he had pneumonia at three months and we had to rush him to the hospital. When we asked the doctor how come he hadn't told us earlier, he said he'd just never seen Down's syndrome* before. The public health nurse here suggested that I have him evaluated again. I don't suppose it'll hurt."

Jeff has continued to have heart problems, and his parents have faced both his physical condition and mental retardation with calmness and wisdom so that Jeff has grown up to be a nice, able young man who does well living at home in his own community.

Dodie and I became friends and partners. She was an experienced primary teacher, while my experience was stronger in working with teenagers and adults. Because she also had a boy younger than Jeffrey, she couldn't work full time yet, but she promised to help me all she could—and did.

---

* Formerly called "mongolism," Down's syndrome is one of the most common causes of mental retardation. It is the result of a defect in chromosome pair 21 which occurs at conception and is characterized by a combination of physical and mental disabilities.

That summer we both worked at a summer camp in the hills of Santa Cruz. The camp was cosponsored by the San Francisco Association for Retarded Children and the special education department of San Francisco State College. Tom Murphy and Rita Mattei, two dynamic special education teachers, codirected the college course and camp operation. For many of the students/counselors this was the first time they had lived with a retarded child or adult around the clock. They found it a strenuous and invaluable experience—one that I am convinced should be a mandated prerequisite for all teachers of children with disabilities. It would bridge impasses in understanding and enhance parent-teacher respect.

Dodie was a cabin counselor for a group of boys and I worked with girls. We never walked. We ran and huffed and puffed up and down hill all day. In the evening, after all the campers were tucked into their cots, those counselors who were working for special education credits gathered in the lodge by the fire to try to tie the day's experiences to the body of theory and methods which Tom and Rita were to impart to us. It didn't work out that way. We'd sit on the floor, huddled in our sweatshirts, and doze off. The two wise professors realized that those reading assignments and anectodal records, which they had at first required, really weren't all-important. What mattered more was for the campers to learn new skills and have a lot of fun under first-class supervision. Whether they came from the wards of state hospitals or the shelter of their own homes, here at camp they were expected to do many things which they had thought they could not do. Camper and counselor alike experienced growth in shocked surprise. And before camp was over, I earned the distinction of having visitors mistake me for a camper, and a camper was assumed to be a counselor. They couldn't tell us apart in our grubby shorts. Hooray!

I returned to Camp La Honda for a second round of credential credits in 1961. This time I served as chief recreation counselor, song leader, organizer of fun and games, and booster of enthusiasm. Our children were allowed to come with me. Barbara camped with the little kids for one week, and Karen and David were junior, junior counselors for the entire stretch.

Rita, the director, ruled that Barbara's cabin counselor was to make believe that I was not there. She wanted Barbara to have the full experience of independence, and she wanted me to function efficiently in my work without parental worries. It worked out well. I rarely saw or heard from Barbara. She'd give me an offhand wave in the dining room or an embarrassed smile as I hoarsely led the singing at the campfire. Except for one evening.

"Come see Barbara—she's crying," came the SOS. I hurried to her cabin and sat by her. She was already tucked into bed. "What's the matter?" I asked. "I want my prayers!" she wailed. So I launched into our " Now I lay me down to sleep" routine that she was used to at home, and she was asleep before I had finished. She was dead tired after trudging up and down those hills all day and just needed a little reassurance.

The camp session turned out to be a mix of work and play for Karen and David. Both of them were messengers deluxe for the director and staff and trotted many miles. Karen, at twelve, was better able to accept direct responsibility for campers than ten-year old David. She could help with dressing and undressing at the swimming pool and in her cabin, and she assisted with arts and crafts. David's major contribution turned out to be his friendship with one of the campers who was a couple of years older than he but about the same size. His friend's disability was barely visible in a camp setting. Both David and he liked little cars. David had brought a supply from home, and the two of them pushed cars along dirt race-tracks for hours. The two boys' easy summer friendship became an affirmation for us all. The alikeness had indeed transcended their supposed difference.

Both Karen and David glowed with pride when Rita rewarded their efforts with ten-dollar salary checks. As a further surprise, the Department of Health, Education and Welfare in Washington, D.C., spun out a Social Security number for David.

Our friends, the Halls, helped mightily with the coordination of these summer ventures. Barbara stayed at their house after her own camp session was finished, while Karen and David and I worked on. They visited me at La Honda one summer, and eight-year-old Ken and nine-year-old Kris were very impressed with it. "When will we be old enough to be counselors at Barbara's camp?" Krissy wanted to know. They got their chance when they were teenagers, after the parent associations in our area of northern California had organized our own camp.

Barbara went to both summer camps for many more years. Just as we had intended, she looked forward to camp as the high point of the year. She was not homesick. She did not catch cold. She did not drown. She walked better and spoke more words because she was excited and had more to talk about.

During her early camp years, she spent an additional week or two with the Halls, who were then living in Fresno. When she was about ten or eleven, we discovered that she was actually able to swim in deep water. When Al and I came to gather up our children, Lloyd Hall asked us to watch Barbara in the pool. "We think she'd be okay in the deep end, but we didn't want to take on the responsibility without you." We went swimming, and soon the two Dads organized a brisk game of water tag. Four adults and a bunch of kids were chasing each other and the ball in and out around the pool. Big splashes and loud hoops and hollers.

"Where's Barbara?" someone asked.

She was calmly floating in the middle of the deep end as if in the eye of a hurricane! Arms around her knees, she was doing a classic Red Cross jellyfish float. I swam up to her anxiously. She was as relaxed as could be. Nice big air bubbles were rising rhythmically around her face, and in between she'd come up for a breath with a smile. She certainly was ready for the deep end, and everyone congratulated her as if she'd swum the English Channel.

Each year when we arrived at camp, we noticed how quickly she turned away from us to a beloved counselor whom she remembered from a previous year. And the reverse happened when we came to get her. Al and I were more excited about the reunion with our little daughter than she seemed to be, as she lingeringly hugged the new friends she had made. Could she be wishing for more love and friendship than we gave her?

When Dodie Scott and I returned to Fort Bragg from our first camp experience in 1960, we were leaner, wiser, and determined to open school. Camp had given me an intensive, firsthand experience in working with children and adults who had a variety of different types and degrees of mental retardation. One week I had three girls in my cabin who were bedwetters, and one of them also had her period! Each morning I had pried myself out of my bunk at the first peep of the sun in order to put dibs on the sunniest branch for drying out soggy sleeping bags. I was not afraid anymore.

Dodie had met many campers with Down's syndrome like her own little boy, and she had seen how much hope there is for their future. I had shared in her joyful surprise during one mid-afternoon quiet period when we were playing restful records for a group of young adults. I had barely turned around from the phonograph when a head came up from the blanket. "That's 'The Sorcerer's Apprentice' by Ducas" announced a so-called retarded camper with authority and lay down again. Dodie and I could hardly believe it.

Dodie was not yet able to work at our new school that first year. Her younger boy needed her at home, she thought, and Jeff could enter later. So I became the sole teacher at a salary of three dollars a day, and she became my most valued advisor. We kept the phone busy with daily recaps and planning sessions.

The school followed the classic pattern of parent-operated ventures. We spoke with an understanding minister, Mr. Kent, who offered us the use of a Sunday school room and a closet for storage. We recruited a few willing volunteers and rounded up the students, most of whom were the children of parent association members and who had never been to school. Some had dropped out or been excluded from public school, and others came via the grapevine. We opened our door at the Presbyterian church in September 1960.

My hands shook a little on that first September morning as I pinned carefully lettered name cards on a cork board and took roll call: "Terry, Penny, Eddie, Russell, Susie, Ernie, Jim, Gary, Helen, Barbara." My ten students sat in a half-circle in front of the board. They were all sizes, shapes, and ages. At six, Barbara was the youngest. Jim towered over her at a lanky eighteen. Some talked a blue streak, while others had few words. They were all eager to learn, and I realized that it would take a mighty versatile program to fit everyone's needs.

"What are you going to call the school?" Karen asked me at home that evening.

"Why call it anything?"

"Mother! You've got to call it something. What if someone asks one of your kids where he goes to school? D'you expect him to say, 'I go to a special class for retarded children in the Presbyterian church?' "

I had to agree. We needed a name. Karen thought of one from local lumbermen's lore. "Call it the Paul Bunyan School," she suggested.

"Paul Bunyan? Why him? He was huge. Our class is small!"

"But Mom—he did the impossible, too," she replied. And so it became the Paul Bunyan School.

From the very start Dodie and I decided that we would run the school program as well as any public school special class. If the daily minimum attendance requirement for such a class was 180 minutes, we would hold school for three hours. Whatever the education code required we would do—only better. When the public schools became ready to take on responsibility for our children, we'd measure up.

Ten in the morning seemed to be a good time to start. Most of our parents had more than one child to get off to school. Most of them lived several miles out of town and had to drive their child to our class. I could vouch for the fact that it was certainly a big rush in the mornings. We set the school day for ten until two in the afternoon.

Barbara loved the commotion. While I tore through the house with a dust mop, washed the breakfast dishes, did a little preparatory supper cooking, and figured out a shopping list, she'd stand with her nose glued to the dining room window until Karen's and David's big yellow schoolbus arrived. Then she'd help me. At six she was unable to put her longing into language, but it was written all over her face that she wished she could go on the bus with them, instead of with me in the old station wagon.

We stayed in that church room from September until the following Easter vacation. We used the room every weekday, and then cleaned and re-arranged it for Sunday school use. A few more students joined our ranks, and many, many volunteers. I had to get up a little earlier each Monday morning, because there were so many teaching materials to be set out before the students arrived.

The Friday afternoon stowaway operation in the hall closet became more and more of a challenge. "This week you're not going to make it, Lotte," Mr. Kent would pronounce as he watched me kneeling on the floor surrounded by boxes, rolls of reading charts, piles of construction paper, arithmetic workbooks, crayons, glue, material scraps, and other treasures that I had scrounged from the public school supply closets. "Oh ye of little faith," I teased him, and then we'd both push the closet door shut. My own papers, lesson plans, and student records I filed in a grocery carton and carried from school to home and back again.

Barbara blossomed. She, too, could now carry home proof of her progress—finger paintings, lined pieces of newsprint with wobbly letters, and even homework. Karen and David drew her into the suppertime sharing period. "How was school today? What did you do?" One word answers grew into two-word sentences, and speech was on its way.

One evening we had invited Father Larsen, the vicar of the Episcopal parish, for supper. Dick Larsen loved all young people and was fond of ours. He brought along a visiting ministerial friend from out of town, whose one arm was so disabled that he could barely use it. "Pass the butter, please," said the friend and proceeded awkwardly to pile it on a muffin. Barbara had been told dozens of times to use a little butter (she has not yet learned this twenty years later), so she watched his performance with great interest. Then —"Too much!" she stated clearly, causing us both embarrassment and pride.

The Paul Bunyan students were highly visible around town that first winter. The church was located on a downtown corner, which lacked open space for outdoor play and exercise. Both teacher and students desperately needed to get out of that crowded room everyday to break the pace and tension of those early experimental weeks. On dry, sunny days we walked five blocks to the slides, swings, and basketball hoops of the city playground.

When it rained, we organized neighborhood field trips. We visited the bakery at doughnut baking time, the train station and the roundhouse, the mill, the firehouse, and even the police station and jail. Then we began making a twice weekly soup and sandwich lunch in the church kitchen and shopped for groceries. "Your children are so well behaved! Why they mind better than my own!" we heard. "Jane is so much quieter when she comes with the class. You know how she screeches when she's with her Mom. See! Gary picked out that can of tomatoes all by himself!" The clerks in the store reflected our pride. It was the start of the kind of awareness and support that our students deserved and needed.

During one of these early shopping trips Barbara really distinguished herself. She was supposed to put some carrots into a bag. All of a sudden she wheeled around and trotted towards me. She held a carrot by the thin end and was swinging it with sort of a whiplike motion to demonstrate its limpness. "Carrots no good, Mom!" she shouted clearly, for the store owner and all the world to hear!

The volunteers who assisted us during those first few months took more of my energy than anything else. It was both a buoying and a draining experience. We knew that the parents of our students deserved a little rest. We did not yet have any transportation for them. Many of them told us that by the time they had driven to school it was almost time to turn around and pick their children up again, so we tried to find volunteers who were nonparents.

This arrangement caused us to do much soul searching. We were being asked to talk about our program. Social and service clubs, fraternal organizations, and study groups, with which Fort Bragg abounded, invited us to speak. Dodie or I accepted all invitations and dashed over during lunch or after school, to tell them about our newfound knowledge. Inevitably someone would ask, "How come you need so many volunteers? Why can't the parents help more?"

It was a tough one. The lack of transportation was easy enough to explain in the beginning, but it was clearly not a major reason. We continued to need many volunteers long after we had provided a volunteer car pool and had ferreted out an obscure paragraph in the education code which stated that superintendents "may" provide bus transportation to private schools. Why couldn't or wouldn't we ask more parents to donate their time?

The honest answer was that they were drained. The anxiety and frustration of having a child whose special needs were not being met had taken all the starch out of most of the parents, and in their defeated state they needed our school program for respite. They needed and deserved a few hours to themselves to charge their batteries.

When we looked at our roster of families, most of them had multiple problems. Several were on welfare and had neither the ability nor motivation to drive their child to school or to take part in the overall planning of our association. One of our students with Down's syndrome also had diabetes. His older sister—the only other child in the family—died of diabetes complications. The death of one man left his widow barely able to cope with the care of our student and a hard-to-manage teenage son. One mother started to have a daytime drinking problem, and an hour after school was out I would try to phone and rouse her so that she could come and pick up her child. Two pairs of brothers were enrolled in our program.

Most of our families were poor. Only a small handful of us had the good fortune to be healthy, energetic, affluent, and "together" enough to carry on the Paul Bunyan School project. We were beginning to understand the message that was put out by our national organization during the Kennedy administration: 85 percent of all mental retardation is the mild form, which is caused by social, cultural, and economic deprivation. This is a huge, long-term problem which our nation still needs to confront.

We continued to recruit volunteers. Their schedule had to be precise and tight. Although helpers could give as little or as much time as they chose, I insisted that they phone me ahead if they were unable to make it so that I could line up a substitute. I encouraged them to ask me questions and assured them that it did not take a degree to teach our students the practical skills which they themselves possessed. I spent hours on the phone each afternoon when I returned home from school, and we developed a fine pool of volunteers—primitively trained but loyal and full of energy.

I had to learn the hard way that there were certain drawbacks to relying on volunteers. You couldn't fire them! So we developed equally primitive criteria for chosing from among the townspeople who answered our invitation to "come see what we are doing—and help."

It all started with the swimming program. I had a hunch, based on my experience as a camp water safety counselor, that our students could learn to swim. It was an activity with which I had overcome my own poor coordination. I thoroughly believed in its therapeutic effect, and besides, we agreed that some of our students needed showers. The municipal pool was funky, but it was indoors and heated. I was surprised at the Recreation Department's lack of opposition. "As long as you're a Red Cross water safety instructor and have plenty of volunteers, why not?" I assured them that we planned to have one adult with each child, and they promised to cover us with their insurance.

We decided to stage a "dry run" in preparation for the great first swim day. We'd walk to the pool and watch the high school coach teach a class. Then we'd show our youngsters the dressing rooms and the showers. Two middle-aged matrons were the scheduled volunteers for the Wednesday before the first Thursday. "Swimming!" they exclaimed in unison. "Don't you think that's too dangerous?" I could have cheerfully strangled them both since several of our students were within earshot, but I confined myself to a mere mutter and tried to maneuver the two women into a corner. There we continued our discussion.

The problem was that both women were so full of good intentions. They had been among the first to step forward when we needed help, and they were dependable, punctual Wednesday helpers. They were also power figures in our small town. Their husbands were prominent businessmen who belonged to the service club that had promised to hold a major fund-raising affair on our behalf. How do you tell such a volunteer that she should think before she speaks? Their personal doubts and apprehensions piled on top of our students' fears and self-doubts were devastating to our students. Since they continued their thoughtless chatter, we learned to prepare for Wednesdays by having plenty of other helpers on board to run interference. We assigned the two stalwarts to neutral tasks away from our most sensitive children. And from then on I screened volunteers.

I asked each one to spend some time at school before I put them on the schedule. I observed their reactions and those of our students towards the potential new helper. Then we'd sit down and talk. "Those poor children!" spoken with tears welling up was a negative cue. I didn't want our children to be pitied. We looked for cheerful, practical, positive people who could instinctively recognize our students' potential for growth. They outnumbered the others by far. And I learned to sidetrack those with negative reactions into helping us in ways which did not involve direct contact with students. We could always use help in our thriftshop, and there was a need for baking cakes for birthdays and holiday parties as well as assistance at our varied fund-raising events.

Someone asked me one day, "What makes a good volunteer for your program, Lotte?" By then we had added high school helpers to our afternoon and weekend recreation program. I noticed that many of them seemed to come from the troubled fringe of the school population: the kind of kids who nowadays might elect to go to alternative school. "I think it has to do with understanding hurt," I said. "Yes, our best volunteers have experienced trouble and know about feeling devalued."

Susan was an exception. She shone at home, on the school campus, and as a volunteer at the Paul Bunyan School, but then her interest had been awakened by having Barbara as a neighbor during their nursery school days. She began delving into mental retardation for a junior high school science report. When she came to ask me about some of the particulars of our school curriculum, she inadvertently taught me a big lesson and radically changed my thinking.

"How come your school is off by itself?" she wanted to know. By then we had moved out of the church and into our own building—a small frame bungalow on a residential side street. I gave Susan my best special education teacher answer: "Shelter, protection from hurt, homelike environment."

She wrote it all down and then looked up. "Do you think Barbara could carry a tray in a cafeteria line?" she asked.

"Yes, now she could. I don't think she could have done it a few years ago, but we ate in a cafeteria in the city not long ago, and she did it there." The question puzzled me. "Why do you ask?"

Her answer came slowly and thoughtfully. "Well then, why couldn't she go to our school? It seems to me that you're protecting us from something we shouldn't be protected from. You don't protect us from crippled children or deaf or blind children. Why do you protect us from retarded children?"

From the mouth of a twelve-year-old, I heard the first mention of "mainstreaming."

The real learning started when we moved the school from the church to Corry Street. Now we had a living-dining room combination, two small bedrooms, a kitchen, a backyard, and a woodshed. We also had fifteen students and volunteers with varied talents, whom I remember with pleasure and gratitude. We did some fancy grouping to accomplish individualized programs and used every inch of space in that small house. From the group of regular volunteers, we chose four women whom we employed to teach fulltime for one week each month. They prepared careful lesson plans and rotated. Dodie's husband and some of our older boys built a wooden deck in the lumpy backyard so that we'd have a level space to dance and exercise in good weather. Various community organizations brought us play equipment. We planted a garden. We placed a cot in the bathtub so that it could double as a "restroom" for high-strung students, provided it wasn't being used for toothbrushing practice or other bathroom activities. We cooked lunch every day now, and the woodshed became a woodworking shop.

The wide ability and age range of our fifteen students put a tremendous load on our program and at the same time kept us from getting into a rut. Our volunteer faculty were able to recognize the students' changing program needs and contributed their own skills and resources to our curriculum. "Helen embroiders so well, couldn't we teach her to hem and sew up pillowcases? My sister-in-law has this old treadle machine that she'd let us use." And we gained a sewing machine. "Eddie is real handy with a splitting axe and a hatchet, and this place is icy cold every morning. Why don't we make him responsible for the kindling for the fireplace and the woodstove?" And soon Eddie was not only preparing the wood, but also setting and lighting the fires, and teaching the younger students.

We were starting to organize three programs under one roof. In the front bedroom I taught the more academic program to students who were older and more advanced in reading and numbers skills. Our four rotating teachers taught the younger crew in the back bedroom. This included Barbara and kept her away from her teacher/mother as much as possible. Actually, the matter of teaching my own child did not bother me too much, having been trained in the British tradition of home teaching for one's own children. All of our students took part in a morning program of exercises, reading, numbers, speech, and lunch preparation.

In the afternoon the older ones branched out into a more vocationally oriented track. By then we knew that the top permissible age for a public school class would be twenty-one. Several of our young men and women were either pushing that age or were already in their early twenties. One or two of them were showing signs of restlessness at going to school with a bunch of little kids. Academic skills bored them, but they did well at practical chores.

A primitive vocational training program evolved naturally. The parent association's fund-raising thrift shop provided an opportunity for sorting donated clothes, washing them in the laundromat, and then ironing. We heard from a friendly nurseryman that leaf mold would sell well to the many commercial fuchsia and rhododendron nurseries on the coast, and this became a project for our young men. Leaf mold results from many layers of pine and fir needles which, when left for years, become a thick springy turf and thus a fine protective mulch for plants. We borrowed a pickup truck, acquired pitchforks and spades, begged for old gunny sacks from the feed store, and went out to harvest the stuff.

A neighbor with paraplegia became one of our most valued teachers. Injured in a woods accident, Oakley Bunner had to be in a wheelchair. He heard of our small woodshop and volunteered to teach carpentry to the older boys. Since he himself had overcome a radical change in his lifestyle and had never babied himself, he wasn't about to pity or overprotect our young men. Twice a week they walked several blocks unescorted to his shop to work with him. Hilja Davis, a respected retired restaurant owner, became the teacher for the thrift shop training program. Both she and Mr. Bunner made fine, firm supervisors a few years later, when the public school system took over the Paul Bunyan School, and the parent association assumed responsibility for the adults' work activity center.

This sort of flexibility was one of the advantages of operating as a private school. There were obvious disadvantages, too. We were forever worrying about money, and scrounging supplies became a bore. While we drooled over catalogues of fancy equipment which we coveted but couldn't afford, there were times when we were inundated with donations which we couldn't use. The public was somehow locked into thinking that all retarded children looked at or made scrapbooks out of old greeting cards. "I've been saving Christmas cards for years and thought you could use them." Of course, we accepted with thanks.

We'd get an urgent call from a store. "Our new wallpaper sample books just came in. If you come right now you can have the old ones, but you'd better hurry and get them today 'cause we've gotta get rid of the old ones." With that someone would dash downtown to pick them up. Wallpaper books came in handy. We took everything during those early years, even if it meant a stealthy trip to the dump at dusk to dispose of unwanted items.

Our school even came to the attention of the producer of *The Russians Are Coming, The Russians Are Coming* when it was being filmed in Mendocino and Fort Bragg. They had a problem with box lunches. Whenever the fog rolled in, which it does often during summertime, they had to send the extras home for the day. What to do with the lunches? I was ready to close school one day, when a truck pulled up and delivered a small mountain of pink cardboard cartons. Each contained a couple of sandwiches, some fruit, a cupcake, and a candy bar. The school refrigerator was a home-sized hand-me-down! I called a couple of friends for help. They came and we sorted, bagged, and then borrowed freezer space. There were many more foggy days and deliveries of pink box lunches, and we were still eating movie cupcakes well over a year later.

Our program grew rounder and richer when Dodie recruited Cindy Trew as a second "curriculum consultant." She, too, was a primary teacher, busily raising a small family before she returned to work. Dodie and Cindy taught me the fine art of making large experience charts for reading lessons. I even found that I could illustrate them with stick figures which helped to tell the story. Together we discovered the value of singing and music for speech development. Tape recorders were like magic mirrors, reflecting little voices saying, "My name is Dan [or John or Helen]. I live in Fort Bragg." Over and over, clearer and clearer.

When it was too rainy to use the deck outside, we exercised indoors. I found a record with peppy music and instructions for calisthenics which could be done between the desks. I set such an enthusiastic example with the arm-fling exercise that next spring my dresses were too tight across my already ample chest, though I had lost three pounds. From then on I faked that exercise!

Dodie and I attended a one-day workshop in the controversial Doman Delacato patterning method. It was designed to train or retrain certain portions of the brain which had been injured in an accident or were underdeveloped. Patterning consisted of early-childhood-type exercises like crawling, or moving the child's arms and legs in alternating left-right flexing and stretching motions many, many times over. Balancing was also stressed and practiced. The assumption was that these movements were related to the development of certain necessary perceptual prereading skills, and so they would eventually improve academic learning. We did not really learn enough in that one day to practice or test the method thoroughly, nor did we have the space in our little house and the money for the required balancing bars and crawling tunnels. We did, however, attempt to teach some of our children to walk up and down the four steps to our schoolhouse with alternate feet and without hanging on to the banister. "Left, right, left, right—let your arms swing!" We practiced once or twice a day, and though we noticed no spectacular reading progress, Barbara and Jane managed to put one foot in front of the other—an improvement over their former one-step approach.

Overall, it just seemed to make sense that the ancient Greeks' theory, "a sound mind in a sound body," would work for our students, too. Along with calisthenics and swimming, dancing became a high point of the week. From simple round and square dances to waltzes and abandoned rock, we tried them all. Don Frye became our smooth and elegant volunteer teacher. Jane was his most talented and graceful partner for the waltz. Norma and Barbara preferred wild drum beats. A couple of the guys were reluctant to get involved in the beginning, but they soon loosened up. Friday afternoons we piled up the tables and desks and chairs and danced. Then we all went home relaxed and smiling.

With the help of my two academic "consultants," we also stumbled onto a form of assessment and evaluation of our students' work. Again, it was Karen and David who tipped us off. "Are you going to give report cards to your kids, Mother?" they wanted to know. By then most of our students were riding public school buses. This represented another small but hard-won victory, and the superintendent of schools was setting a mighty precedent by providing school bus transportation for pupils of a private school. Karen and David thought it would terrible for Barbara and her schoolmates to go home empty-handed on report card day.

This launched a process that was time consuming and hard work. Soul searchingly, we began to clarify our aims and objectives for our students. We threw out letter grades in favor of statements of skills, broadly grouped in the areas of social skills, physical and emotional health, work habits, recreational activities, and skills for economic self-sufficiency.

Under social skills we might comment on Jane's poise

116

and charming manner of greeting visitors. Barbara received credit for new words and sentences. Table manners, grooming, and speech were given specific, detailed, comments.

Under the heading of physical and emotional health, we paid attention to coordination and reported to parents on improvements in specific exercises and dances. Everybody had to brush his or her teeth after lunch. One girl had screamed and fussed at the mere sight of a toothbrush. I had to take her in a vise grip and do it for her. She was now able to do it herself—gingerly! Fingernails looked cleaner and shorter, and we said so on the report card.

The section on work habits included comments on promptness, cleanliness, getting along with others, and following directions. We were deliberately building these skills even with little ones. "Following Directions" was a favorite game. "Take this pencil, John, and give it to Mrs. Moise. Then open the front door. Come back inside and bring a book to Mrs. Cain." The report card would state that "John can now follow three, or four, or even five directions in a row."

Under recreational activities we listed accomplishments in crafts (cutting with scissors, pasting neatly, coloring within lines, finger painting and clay sculpting), swimming, bowling, and simple table games which took the place of outdoor games on many rainy afternoons. Actually, there was little need to comment on bowling, since their score sheets—carried home triumphantly—gave ample proof of phenomenal progress. Jeff and several other little ones began their bowling careers by placing the ball between their crouched legs and pushing it down the alley. Before long they were standing and swinging the ball and proudly pointing to spares and strikes on the score sheet. In time many of them garnered trophies at special state tournaments and far outbowled me. Swimming reports were equally impressive. We recruited many volunteers from the ministerial association and from the police department, and with their patience and encouragement most of our students eventually became deep water swimmers.

There was a long list of items under the heading of skills for economic self-sufficiency. Terry learned to tell time by the half and quarter hour. Ernie and Richard were learning to read real books. Barbara could recognize "stop" and "go." Gary was able to distinguish "men" from "women." Jim could endorse a check with a legible signature. Everyone was improving in the many tasks having to do with clean-up, cooking, gardening, and woodwork. We tried to teach all the children to "tie up the bundle" (do a job from beginning to end). Rather than handing them the broom, we asked them courteously to fetch it, do the job, and put it away. Time and time again we reminded ourselves and each other that we intended to relate all learning to the children's future needs.

We had objectives for the parents, too, and sometimes we worked with parents almost as much as we did with the students. We realized that it took some of them years to look at their problems squarely and to do the right thing for and with their son or daughter. On a four-page paper entitled "Notes for Paul Bunyan School Teachers and Helpers," we listed the following objectives for parents:

> To accept their child the way he or she is.
> To accept the child's limitations and not to push the child beyond them.
> To see the child's positive qualities and talents and to make the most of them.

To interpret our program to other homes and the whole community.

To face the future.

All of this took hours, but it was worth it. We invited the parents to come to school for individual conferences, during which we talked with them about their son's or daughter's strong and weak spots and urged them to support our school program with home practice. Then we folded the reports into small manila envelopes straight from the public school supply closet, and the students carried them home "just like other kids."

9 Balloons And Bubbles

WE SENT UP LOVELY BALLOONS and experienced lots of burst bubbles during the first four years of the Paul Bunyan School. The students burst most of the bubbles, but all of us—students, teachers, volunteers, parents, and towns-people—lofted new concepts and ideas like lovely bright balloons.

I graduated from a cardboard grocery carton to an old green file cabinet which locked. In it we kept confidential files on each of our students. They contained report cards, information on IQ scores (natch!), results of the Vineland Social Maturity Scales, parent release forms for having publicity photos published, and permission slips for swimming, field trips, and the use of potentially dangerous tools such as power lawnmowers and saws.

As I came to know our students as real people, their IQs became chimerical. When new helpers and visitors would ask me about a student's IQ, I often blanked. I was not getting forgetful or trying to make a point. Those numbers were simply becoming nonvital statistics. The planning which made the complex school program function—who was assigned certain tasks, which skills were missing, and how we might recruit another helper to solve a specific problem—those were my uppermost concerns.

From the start we engaged in vocational forecasting. We felt we had no choice. Several of our students were big, active country boys with little liking for book learning. The sooner we could move them towards earning a living, the better. Tall, lanky Jim, for example, hated to sit still. Contrary to what we had been told in college ("trainable students are less aware of their deficits than those who are educable"), Jim seemed extremely sensitive about his previous academic failures. And yet he was an anchor man when it came to doing chores and giving practical advice. On our very first field trip I realized that I'd be much better off lost in the woods with Jim than with most of my friends. He was wonderfully dependable, resourceful, and responsible for our younger students. Even during the early sixties, when environmental deprivation had hardly been heard of, Dodie and I expressed our hunch that his so-called mental retardation and that of several of our other students resulted from their impoverished background, total lack of cultural stimulation at home, and poor health care and nutrition.

For Easter that first spring we received one of our questionably useful gifts from a pet store owner. He came to school in person, bearing a cardboard box. (We welcomed spontaneous visits. Though we realized that they were a little distracting to our students and consumed staff time, they paid off by telling the townspeople about our program. Nobody was pushing us with precise curriculum expectations, so we considered these visits as time well spent.) I barely glanced inside the carton and thanked our guest for the donation. Later, I discovered that the box was filled with moving multicolored fluff. The well-meaning merchant had given us a half dozen chicks dyed for Easter.

They soon outgrew their colored down and turned into plain white hens—noisy, hungry, thirsty, smelly, and dirty. We placed a hand-me-down chicken pen in the far corner of the backyard, and Jim became their keeper. He did a tremendous job. Before I came to school early in the morning, he had already emptied the trays and changed the feed and water. One day I complimented him. "You're doing a good job, Jim. I've been thinking I might talk to one of our neighbors about you. He has a chicken ranch. I may be able to get you a job there."

Jim looked glum and shook his head.

"Don't you like working with chickens, Jim?"

He continued shaking his head. "Nah, Moise. I *hate* chickens. I wanna work with cars!"

There went the first bubble. Who was planning for whom? I was obviously caught in the same stereotyped thinking as the rest of the world. "Let's let blind people weave baskets!" What right did I have to plan for Jim's future without considering his interests? We gave away those chickens, and Jim eventually went to work for a body and fender business.

We had begun our school program with a four-hour day because the attention span of "trainable" students was not supposed to extend beyond that. Within a very few months we found that day far too short. Our students required so many varied activities that we soon stretched the school day to six hours. Of course, the students stretched right along with the schedule.

The reading program turned out to be another surprise. I had been taught to teach only survival words such as stop and go, hot and cold, men and women, and so forth, but both Richard and Ernie were clearly interested in stories. They moved rapidly from flash cards with single words through primers to real books. I was pretty excited by this unexpected breakthrough and began to lean more heavily on our most able students. One day I was urging Ernie to hurry up with his reading. He looked up from his book accusingly: "I'm doing my best, Moise!" The student had told his teacher to ease the pressure. From then on we scheduled time for reading "just for fun." We read aloud storybooks and interesting local newspaper items, and Ernie clearly liked Peter Pan best of all. That is how I learned another lesson.

He came to school one morning with a big bruise on the side of his face.

"What happened?" we all asked.

"Well, I wanted to try again," he said.

"Try what, Ernie?"

"Fly like Peter Pan. I climbed a tree. I wanted to fly down like him."

There went another bubble. Who was it who had tried to teach us that retarded youngsters have no imagination?

There was also the matter of teaching in the here and now, remember? "Nothing beyond the immediate neighborhood will be meaningful to your students." Nonsense! In dozens of small ways we began to widen our students' horizons, because they showed us that they were able to range farther afield.

During one summer vacation Barbara proved that we were on the right track. My mother had invited me to go to Hawaii with her during the ten days that Barbara would be at summer camp. While Al and the children were seeing us off, Barbara piped up, "Bring me a funapple, Mom!"

"A what-did-you-say?"

"A funapple," she repeated emphatically, making a circular motion with her hands.

"She means a pineapple," David interpreted. "She knows they have 'em there."

And after we were all home again, I had to interrupt whatever I was doing repeatedly to respond to yells of panic from the living room where Barbara was watching TV. "Mom! Come quick! Hawaii on TV!" And sure enough, there'd be a hula girl under a palm tree, a surfer, or a catamaran. Barbara clearly connected all of them with Hawaii.

We began to reach beyond our own neighborhood with school field trips. The financial wizards on the school's advisory board shook their heads in disapproval at our extravagant requests. "Next you'll be wanting to take them to the San Francisco Zoo," they clucked. Dodie and I bit our lips and touched knees under the table. That is exactly where we wanted to go—to the zoo and to the planetarium, to Disneyland and to snow country, out on a boat and up in a plane. "Here and now" was for the birds.

We did a great deal for our students beyond providing them with a stimulating learning environment. We tried to enrich their lives with sentiment and dignity. Every one of them had a birthday party with a cake and candles and a carefully thought-out individual present. Santa Claus came at Christmas time and brought each person a gift. We became so caught up in doing and giving that we almost forgot one very important point: it is demeaning to be always on the receiving end. "Allbody" (a word Barbara coined) enjoys the glow of giving.

One day I returned to the state institution where I had served a six-week apprenticeship for academic credit towards my special credential. As I visited one of the wards, my guide pointed out a young woman and said, "Something interesting happened to me with Shirley the other day. There's this volunteer lady who takes some of our girls to town for a treat once in a while. I went along to chaperone. They had a wishing well in the teashop, and the lady gave Shirley a coin to throw in. She said, 'You're supposed to make a wish, Shirley,' and then, 'What did you wish for?' Do you know what Shirley said? 'I wish I could treat someone to a soda someday!' ''

Among our students it was Richard who first expressed the human need to do for others. Our school district provided a home teacher for five youngsters with physical disabilities. Their teacher approached me to ask if they might use the backyard of the Paul Bunyan School for their annual get-together and party. Her boys wanted to have a wheelchair baseball game, with their mothers running the bases as the boys batted from their chairs. "Why couldn't we do it, Mrs. Moise? Why couldn't we do the running for them?" Richard wanted to know. And so it happened—a fine two-inning softball game, a picnic, and a few songs to wind up the day. Richard had a warm smile on his face which clearly expressed his joy at being on the giving end for a change.

Later, one of our young men made this point even more clearly. Bob was a moody young man with a temper. On one of those days when nothing went right for him, I heard the work supervisor reprimand him and Bob blew his stack. I walked outside with him to help him cool off. We stood on the steps and talked about the situation. Nothing seemed to cut his gloom. "Hey, Bob," I tried. "I saw Mr. Bunner on my way to work this morning. He says he has almost finished straightening the spokes on your bike wheel. You should have it back by tomorrow." I knew that Bob's bike was his prize possession and thought the news would cheer him. "I don't care!" he burst out, "and I'm sick and tired of being helped!"

The teachers of the Paul Bunyan School learned many more concepts from the students and from each other. We learned that students have the right to move on and up. When Richard first entered a public school special class, we missed him terribly. He was so articulate and bright and cheerful. How would we ever do the morning "share and tell" period without him? To add insult to injury, he avoided speaking to me now when we met downtown! He was so proud at going to regular school that his former association with us embarrassed him. As he grew in self-esteem and poise, he was able to chat with me again, as we met in the downtown library where he was checking out armfuls of books. Next he became manager of the high school football team and glowingly told me about it. He moved to a neighboring town to live in a group home with other residents capable of being trained for living on their own. At first he worked in a sheltered workshop, but now he is employed as a teachers' aide in an activity center where the students have fairly severe disabilities and special needs. Richard lives in his own apartment and manages his own affairs with counseling support as the need arises. There is an organization in our four-county rural area which is trying to develop a full range of living arrangements for persons with developmental special needs. Recently, Richard was appointed to its board of directors while I was the chairperson, and during that year we proudly met once a month as fellow planners. He contributed much from his personal experience and wisdom, and I knew that our letting go had freed him to grow.

Not all of our students moved away from us so early. Some graduated to the work activity center, a program for young adults run by our parents' group, and we experienced surprises there, too. One young man kept arriving at the center earlier than anyone else. He'd wait for a staff person to open the place, and one morning he said, "If you let me have a key, I could open up and have the place all warm by the time we get started." Consternation! It seemed unusual, almost inappropriate, for a "client" to assume a "staff" responsibility. We thought about it and then gave him this small but significant assignment.

Another young man asked if he could attend our weekly staff meetings. "I'm real interested in a lot of that stuff— and our money troubles." Surprise again! It had truly become "our" center. He felt a part of it, and if we were honestly expecting him to manage on his own in the community, perhaps it wouldn't hurt to expose him to our money worries and other concerns. Both these young men began to attend staff meetings, and gradually the staff/ client differences eroded to the benefit of us all. We all had problems, which we tried to solve jointly. These particular young men are living on their own now. One of them occasionally gives me a breezy wave from his pickup truck as we pass on the street. The other is married and touches base more often in a neighborly, friendly way. He and his wife still have problems, but they know where to go for help—and do so—just like the rest of us.

It took many small happenings to strengthen my belief in community living. One afternoon, when Barbara was still a small girl, we stopped to see a woman who has an enormous birthmark covering her mouth and chin. I had long admired Kathryn's poise and presence at social gatherings and PTA meetings, but I had not prepared Barbara for this occasion. Her eyes were full of question marks. Kathryn was a jump ahead of me. "Let Barbara ask, Lotte," she said, as she noticed my restraining hand on my child's arm. "It looks strange and different to her." And to Barbara she patiently explained the nature of her birthmark and even encouraged her to touch her face.

It dawned on me that day that if Kathryn could run the gauntlet of thoughtless stares and comments, perhaps Barbara and her peers would learn to do the same.

Another time, I needed to leave town suddenly for an emergency meeting in the county seat and could not reach my regular baby-sitters. I phoned my friend Joanne.

"Could Barbara stay with you for just a few hours after school today?"

My question brought forth a hesitant "yes."

"Please tell me frankly if it's not convenient, Joanne."

"It's convenient, all right," she said. "I'm going to be home anyway, but I'm having Bluebirds, and I'm afraid one of them might hurt Barbara's feelings."

"Never mind that! I'll bring her over in a little while if it's okay."

All the way over the hill and home from the meeting, I thought of Joanne's misgivings. I recalled the early days of our parent movement, when we had scored points with legislators and administrators by telling them, "Our children are more like others than they are different." Was not then the logical extension of this premise that we now had to take a chance on occasional hurt feelings for our children with disabilities, just as we do for our other children?

When I picked up Barbara that evening, she looked happy and content. Joanne told me what a good girl she had been, and added, "I do hope that nobody said anything mean to her." I stood fast and told her of my newly gained awareness. However much I appreciated her sensitivity and concern, I was quite sure now that we would not be able to shield our children from real life. If we wanted our children to live outside of institutions in their home communities, they would run the risk of being hurt or taunted. For the first time I had tumbled onto the concept of risk taking, which Robert Perske later found to be the cornerstone of Scandinavian programs.

We did not learn all our lessons from our own children or our students. At times it took expert advice from "old pros" in the field of mental retardation to set us straight. In 1963 Dodie and I were worrying about our students' adulthood. Where and how would they live when their parents were gone? Perhaps we could persuade someone to donate a few acres and then get some wealthy angels to erect a few buildings. Could we start a farm operation and combine it with a home for adults? We directed our questions to the source of all wisdom and wrote a letter to Dr. Gunnar Dybwad, who was at the time the executive director of the National Association for Retarded Children.

I wax sentimental at the mention of his name and that of his wife Rosemary. Both are giants in their field, but they are far from inaccessible. Over the years they have inspired thousands of parents in countries all over the world with their courage and tenacity. When they left our national association in the sixties, they worked with an international health organization in Switzerland for several years as advisors. Afterwards, they returned home to teach at Brandeis University in the Florence Heller Graduate School. Gunnar twinkles when he teaches and pounds the lectern when he testifies. He is a vehement spokesman at congressional hearings and in courts of law, as he supports legislation and lawsuits that affirm the citizen rights of people with disabilities. Rosemary supports him as a research and resource assistant. She answers letters and is responsible for the creation of the International League of Societies for the Mentally Handicapped. Together they helped me—"a mere parent"—in my wobbly early efforts of writing about Barbara. When the bureaucratic scene in California begins to get me down, I can phone and find them in the faculty lounge of their university at ungodly hours of the night.

So it was with Dodie's and my request for advice in 1963. Gunnar fired back the following reply.

> Lifetime security cannot be bought for any mortal being, be he sick or well, brilliant or retarded. We can attempt to provide, and his parents have a responsibility to do so, but I want to speak very frankly. It seems to me that in some of your planning there seems to be implied a greater desire for "peace of mind" on your part as parents than a genuine understanding of what a retarded person should be assured first of all—an opportunity to achieve his fullest potential in life.
>
> The needs of mentally retarded individuals differ sharply. The fact that twelve children age 8 to 16 years are now in a privately sponsored class by no means allows us to predict that 20, 15, or even 10 years from now these twelve children have the same needs which can be or should be accommodated in the same setting. For some of them, undoubtedly, the facility you picture (*whatever* your picture may be) may be just the right thing, but for others both the location and the type of facility will prove to be an unnecessary restriction on their God given right to lead as full a life as they are capable of living. . . .

Let me make myself clear. It might be quite possible for your group to start a residential facility
just as long as the various members of your group
are not entertaining the fallacious idea that by so
doing they can count on a permanent haven for
their particular child.

We heard Dr. Dybwad's message. We dropped the idea
of creating a premature "haven" and concentrated on the
school program.

It wasn't all smooth sailing at school. We had to make
hard choices when our skills and resources proved to be
inadequate. One of our early students was a girl who had
tremendous, frequent, and uncontrolled seizures. The
other children seemed less upset by them than were the
adults, but in addition to this and her mental retardation,
she acted like a little whirling dervish. Because we had
minimal access to either medical or psychological consultation services, we sadly decided that we could not
keep her in our program. We hated the feeling of ad-
mitting our failure, but we sent her home again.

We also ran into difficult situations working with parents. We knew that Ann could learn to use a knife and
fork, brush her teeth, and put on her clothes. She did all of
these things at school, but her mother would not or could
not help her practice these skills at home. We bootlegged
the services of the county schools' psychologist for one
afternoon, so that he might counsel with both of Ann's
parents. They came, but it seemed that his advice ran like
water off a duck's back. Ann has grown into a tall, good-
looking young woman. She has come a long way, but not
nearly far enough. She still lives at home with her parents,
and Mama still dances to her tune.

John's mother was another difficult person. I pushed

131

her hard, perhaps too hard, to work with her son. She never cooperated with us, and after a couple of years I learned to accept the reality. She was as tough as a brick wall, hostile, and not to be fooled with. All her life had been rough and uphill, and I am sure that she viewed my snug little family and "professional" motherhood as a threat. I became the target of her irrational outbursts, and John had to return to a state institution for several years.

One boy's father ran us off his land with a shotgun! Dodie and I had driven out to try one more time to get the old man's permission for his son to have his adenoids and tonsils removed. Joe already had a 50-percent hearing loss in one ear, and the other was failing, too. He had an astigmatism which should have been corrected long ago, but his father stubbornly refused to give permission for these procedures. "Just think of what this will do for your son's future," we pleaded. "It may make the difference between his being able to stand on his own two feet, or being dependent for life!" The shotgun was all the answer we needed. The boy never had surgery.

The county superintendent of schools crossed the mountain in 1964 to inform us that there was now sufficient funding to make us a proper county school. They would paint the Corry Street house inside and out. We'd get new linoleum, much-needed equipment, and a standard salary for the teacher and aides. After four years of skimping and scrounging on our own, we should have been overjoyed, but we were not. What would happen to our constantly changing, free-wheeling curriculum? Would we still be able to declare impromptu holidays and go on trips to the beach at the drop of a hat? Would we be allowed to enroll tiny tots, not even toilet trained, to enjoy music, commotion, and social contact for a few hours each week? Most of all, we worried about the young adults who by now were older than the top allowable age of twenty-one. They were already working as adults several hours a day in our thriftshop, sifting and bagging leaf mold for sale, and doing carpentry projects. Would they now have to be excluded from the county program and go home to sit around as they had done before? "Over our dead bodies!" we said, and we were reluctant to trade our independence and flexibility for the security of the good superintendent's umbrella.

Ray Hudson, a coworker from the neighboring parent association in the county seat, came over to talk sense into our heads. In Ukiah the county schools had been operating a school program for several years. Great harmony prevailed between the parents and the school. Perhaps our program was a little more varied, a bit more creative, Ray conceded, but how long would we be able to sustain the tremendous effort which our program required, fund raising and all? He had a point there. And why not let the public schools assume the responsibility that they rightfully should? Were not our children entitled to a public school education just like others? And should my assistants and I not receive a salary commensurate with our qualifications? And then came the clincher! If our association handed over the operation of the Paul Bunyan School to the county, we would be free to take the next step—a work-training program for those of our adults who had outgrown school and were ready for a program appropriate to their age.

That was the turning point. We went under the county umbrella in the fall of 1964. The school continued in the same little house for a while longer and is now located on a regular Fort Bragg school district campus. The work activity center was begun the following year, and it is still vigorously supported by the parent association. We had taken a giant step towards the dream of a continuum of programs and services for the disabled citizens of our town.

10 *The Six Rs*

MEANWHILE, LIFE CONTINUED at our house on Sherwood Road. I look back now and wonder how I ever mustered the energy to do justice to both the school house and the home house. Even shopping lists became confusing. "Is this peanut butter supposed to be for our house or for the school?" I was forever asking Barbara if it was okay to borrow one of her toys or books or puzzles or records to take to school until I realized that I was violating her right of possession. Christmas came, and she was pulling her new red wagon around the house when she turned to me and asked, "Keep this home, Mom?" I got the message.

Without Al's and the children's cooperation and the support of our babysitters and friends, we might not have "hung together" as a family. We all knew of marriages that had split up under the stress of a disabled child. We heard about children who felt overwhelmed and embarrassed by a disabled sibling who seemed to deprive them of their parents' love and attention. I would be lying if I gave the impression that Al and I never fought or that our children did not cause us pain. But we survived, and now I can see how we learned, what we learned, and from whom.

It was Barbara who taught us to listen and learn about her needs. Like a Jack-in-the-box, she popped out of her "trainable" cubbyhole and blew my neat professional preconceptions to the four winds. Now that these constraints are gone, I can recognize the six Rs which helped our house become a home: right to respect, regard for differences of opinion, room for differences, risk taking, responsibility, and readiness for role changes.

First there was the *right to respect.* Respect means to "value" and "to be worthy of esteem." Between mates in marriage it is considered a foregone conclusion. Respect can grow, even when passion and romantic love have cooled. But when is it time to respect our children? Is it ever too early to see them as persons?

Once I came into David's room and found him sitting on his bed, doing nothing at all, after I had told him to change his clothes "right now!" When I burst out in anger at his apparent laziness, he looked at me earnestly and said, "Mom, I need to have some time to think."

Karen, an A student, doggedly tried to overcome her poor coordination. Starting with her tiny tricycle, then stilts, later a bike, tumbling, diving, and mastering her big, stubborn horse, she irritated us to the point of anger with her persistence. It took us years to realize that she was trying so hard because she was hell-bent to overcome what she experienced as her own handicap.

Barbara's low-gear rate of progress led us naturally from the high expectations we had taken for granted to generous praise and applause. I can still see her—feet straddled wide, hands clutching the clips of her coveralls—taking her first real steps at age two years and four months. Each new word in her vocabulary became a cause for family celebration. Barbara clearly told me of her own awareness of her handicap when she was about five years old and still talking in abbreviated sentences. She was in the kitchen, helping me peel hard-boiled eggs. As she handed me a finished one, I patted her on the head and congratulated her on being a fine kitchen helper. She shook her head and stuck out her lower lip.

"You don't want to be a kitchen helper, Barbara?" I asked. "What do you want to be when you grow up?"

"I wanna read like Karen and David," was her reply.

It was probably the longest sentence of her life. I knew then that she was indeed aware of her condition, and that, if we truly respected her as a human being she had the right to frank explanations of her impairment and discussions of its implications for her later life.

Regard for differences of opinion was not easily come by in our family. Al and I agreed on certain basics such as politics, religion, and money management, but we disagreed on such sensitive issues as whether claiming a veteran's exemption on property is honorable and whether hot cereal for breakfast every morning is mandatory. We thought we had to present a united front to our children on all issues, and we expected them to echo our opinions automatically.

One day when Karen was only about five, she startled me by asking the meaning of the word "divorce."

"It's when a mummy and daddy don't get along," I explained, "and then maybe they decide not to live in the same house anymore. They fight a lot."

"Like you and Daddy?"

I was appalled. "What gives you that idea? We don't fight!"

"You do too!" Karen countered. "Like you say a word is spelled c-a-t and Daddy says c-e-t and then you go and look it up in a book."

David, the product of two parents who had loyally and

enthusiastically served in the military during World War II, was an avowed pacifist at age eight. At ten, he caused a heated discussion at the supper table when he challenged the value of daily pledging allegiance to the flag in school. Later he startled us with the question, "Do you think the kids in school in Russia are told that everything is best in their country, too?"

During our children's adolescence differences of opinion became the order of the day and ranged from hitchhiking to hotpants, from beards to booze. These were turbulent years, not without worry or anger, but they prepared us for Barbara's emancipation. First she wanted to grow her hair long like her sister. Then she began to gripe about having to ride on the yellow school bus with all the little kids. Finally, she announced in loud and clear tones: "I wanna go somewhere!"

With that, Barbara joined the dissonant chorus, and we realized that home is a good place to air your views, be they ever so outrageous. Gradually we learned to hear each other out—to listen and to accept. As we heard our children's different points of view on all sorts of topics, we learned that they were indeed widely differing people and that their home life was preparing them for an ever-shrinking world full of persons of infinite variety.

Room for differences thus became another component of our family's functioning. As we cheered Barbara for every new skill, we grew in tolerance of each other's short suits. It became acceptable for Mom to be poor at sewing and dense at threading movie projectors. Karen was rated as sloppy in the kitchen but a venturesome cook. David's spelling was purely phonetic, but he was an excellent driver. Father, well, Father remained "perfect"!

We were also learning that our house had space enough

for different people. When Joe the woodcutter and Marie, his wife, lost their cabin to a fire, Al invited them to stay with us. It was a holiday weekend, and our house was already full with our children and friends—college kids, an engineer, and a schoolteacher. I was irritated by the additional influx, and, looking at the total scene from the perspective of a hostess, it was a strange combination of guests. We were out of spare beds and even the living room floor was full, so Joe and Marie had to roll out sleeping bags in the dining room. I could smell their pungent odor of stale smoke, sweat, and booze. Early the next morning I woke up to the sound of an axe on wood. Joe was outside splitting firewood from large redwood rounds and stacking it neatly. This was his trade and the most valuable contribution he could make to our household. I felt warmly grateful to him. At breakfast Barbara turned to Marie, a women in her late thirties, and asked, "Do you go to school?"

"No," was the answer.

"You can come to my school with me tomorrow," Barbara offered. She had picked up on Marie's condition with deadly accuracy before any of the rest of us had had time to observe it. Marie did not read, and academically she was not very able.

It was this kind of warmth and perception that influenced many of the young people who came to our youth hostel. At times, it did seem like a youth hostel because during Karen's and David's school and college years, both felt free to invite their friends home without making reservations beforehand. In the late sixties I was also beginning to meet members of the Youth California Association for the Retarded, and when they came to "rap," they rolled out their sleeping bags on our living room floor during overflow periods. Having these young people in our home led to a two-way enrichment process. Barbara grew greatly in self-esteem because they made her feel that she was one of them. They, on the other hand, were profoundly moved by her, and a remarkable number chose to enter a field of human services.

I treasure a letter from a young woman who heard me share my concerns for Barbara's future at a meeting of youth delegates at a convention. "What really brought some tears," she wrote, "was when you mentioned your child and who will take care of her if something happens to you. I just wanted to say, Mrs. Moise, there are lots of people who love her and we won't let anything happen to her. I had to get it out, 'cause I can't stand for someone to feel bad when it comes to the love of a handicapped child."

Another young friend, Barbara Jessing, has grown from a youthful partner on the California scene to an outstanding colleague on whom I lean for advice. When we first met in 1968, she was a college student, working her way through the University of California. She was a counselor at a special summer camp and also had a job in a residential facility. As an officer of the Youth California Association, Barbara insisted that they not "serve the retarded" but work on their behalf and with them. While I was on the board of directors of the California Association for the Retarded, she became the first voting youth delegate to this body, and I was increasingly impressed with her quiet perseverance and wisdom.

As soon as we returned from Denmark and Nebraska in 1971, Barbara phoned me. "Don and Paula and I would like to hear about your trip. Would it be okay if we come the weekend after Thanksgiving?" Of course it was okay. I was as eager to talk about our experiences as they were to hear about them. "Too bad that you can't afford to go to Denmark," I said, "but perhaps you could make it to Nebraska next summer." Right then and there we phoned Bob Perske in Omaha. "How would you like some out-standing young volunteers from California next summer? If they can get themselves there on their own, and you give them free room and board in your group homes, they could swing it."

It actually happened that way. The Three Musketeers in two rickety old cars trekked to Nebraska in 1972. Paula Karutz, who had graduated with a special teaching credential, stayed in Omaha for two years. She returned to California and is applying her expert sheltered workshop teaching experience as a respected staff member of a fine San Diego program for adults with developmental disabilities. A married couple from Omaha, who were her students there, still come to spend their annual vacation with her in California.

Don, whose sister has mental retardation, returned to finish his degree in sociology in San Francisco and then decided to go into business with his father.

Barbara Jessing is still in Nebraska and working on the counseling staff of the now internationally famous ENCOR (Eastern Nebraska Community Office of Retardation) program. She may return to California one of these years, and when she does, those with developmental disabilities and their parents will be the richer for her presence.

Risk taking was something that Al and I took for granted as a right of our older children. The first ride on a slide, the first night away from home, a bus trip alone, a date with a boy, the driver's license. What made it so much harder to watch Barbara take chances? Perhaps it was that while we had normal expectations of success for

141

Karen and David, Barbara's diagnosis of mental retardation scared us into expecting failure. Once we recognized that risk taking is a prerequisite for learning, we were better able to let go.

So Barbara learned to light her father's pipe and later the fire in the grate. To go on errands to the neighbor's and later on the bus by herself. She learned to swim in deep water and to pour hot coffee. Certain learnings, such as crossing busy street corners and riding escalators, we delegated to someone less personally involved and with a stronger nervous system!

In 1962 David voluntarily took part in one of these risk-taking ventures. I was planning my fourth and last partial summer away from home, this time as a student professional assistant at Sonoma State Hospital. Edith Hall had invited our children to come to Fresno for a couple of weeks, but Karen declined. She did not want to leave her beloved horse, Chips, who was a relatively new member of our extended family, and besides, at thirteen she was old enough to try cooking for herself and Dad for a while. David and Barbara were dying to go, but we saw no way of getting them there since I was unable to drive them down and Al was loaded with work.

"Do you think that David is old enough to handle this?" Al asked.

"He's eleven and pretty hep about transportation," I said, "but I wouldn't want him to feel that he has to do it. We could always ask him, though." So we did.

"How would you feel about taking Barbara down to Fresno on the Greyhound with you? It would mean a change in San Francisco and then going straight through."

David thought a while. "It's okay with me," he said, "except what do I do when she has to go to the bathroom?"

That was a problem. It would take about twelve hours, including the transfer, to get to Fresno. Although Barbara's bladder was exceptionally well disciplined, I had a nagging doubt. In the San Francisco depot, the women's toilets are up a flight of stairs. A couple of stalls are free, but the rest have coin slots. This might confuse her. "Well," we told him, "you should probably pick out a motherly looking lady who's going upstairs, and ask her to help your little sister. And then be sure to stay right there so you don't lose her when she comes down." He agreed to do that.

Barbara fooled him, though. She claimed she didn't have to go in San Francisco and steadfastly maintained the same at every stop on the way south. She performed better than a camel, and poor David, who was unaware of his sister's amazing holding capacity, worried all the way. When they got off the bus in Fresno, Barbara turned to Edith and said, "Hi! I've gotta go wee-wee!"

Al and I sometimes wondered how Karen and David felt about having a little sister with a problem, but we talked to each other about this more than we did with them. Occasionally we made executive decisions about their taking Barbara along with them "because it's only fair"; at other times we asked them, as we did with the Fresno trip. If they felt put upon, I don't remember their saying so.

Karen's teenage efforts to establish her identity and independence were more turbulent than those of David, perhaps because she was older and he learned from her mistakes. It hurt to watch her flounder, but with the help of professional counseling, we learned to look at ourselves squarely and our relationships mellowed. Barbara did not seem to be the direct cause of these upsets. We knew of many families who had no children with special developmental needs who also underwent turbulent teenage times.

When Karen was in her senior year in high school, she began to invite Barbara to come along to occasional folk dance recitals and parties. "She's like an icebreaker for me, Mom. I'm lousy at meeting people. But when Barbara is with me, she walks right up, shakes hands, and introduces herself. 'My name's Barbara,' she'll say. 'What's yours? What did you get for Christmas?' From then on, it's easier for me."

David, now that he's twenty-nine, remembers it this way: "It felt a little weird having a sister who was different, and who was being brought along to everything like a regular family member, but then I felt different anyway when I was in grade school and high school. Because Karen and I were smart, and too fat, and not athletes."

Nowadays we have a better awareness of the emotional needs of siblings of children with disabilities, and it is possible to bring them together with others in the same situation for supportive group counseling.

Apparently David's and Karen's discomfort had changed to confidence by the time they went off to the University of California at Santa Cruz—Karen in 1967 and David two years later.

Karen invited Barbara to spend a week with her on campus during her freshman year. Tucked away safely in a small dormitory room with her sleeping bag, Barbara was allowed to accompany her sister to some classes and seminars. At other times she stayed in the dorm, listened to records, and visited up and down the hall. The entire floor of students looked after her. Two years later David also wanted her to spend a week with him. This time Barbara was stashed away in a boys' dorm. David and his roommate constructed a temporary sleeping loft in their beamed, high-ceilinged room. They slept on the platform while Barbara was down below. She returned home from each of these visits more alert than ever before, with a noticeable increase in self-motivation and a rush of new words and concepts.

It was on one of these Santa Cruz trips that we first became aware of Barbara's extraordinary intuition. In 1968, when she was fourteen and David seventeen, we asked David to pick up his sister at the end of her stay at Santa Cruz. He was proud owner of a hard-earned car and glad of every opportunity to drive it. Grandma Mud was living in Fort Bragg by then, and at almost ninety, she was a little frail. That Saturday a friend invited Al and Mud and me to dinner. During dinner Mud suddenly looked uneasy. Her right hand wouldn't hold anything and one side of her face looked droopy. We took her home, helped her to bed, and called the doctor. It was a very mild stroke, he said, not much more severe than the light fainting spells she'd had from time to time. "Stay in bed tomorrow, Mud," he ordered, "and don't worry about your hand. Two or three days of rest and you'll be as good as new."

When David and Barbara rolled in on Sunday evening, the first words out of Barbara's mouth were, "What's the matter with Mud? Is Mud okay?" I was too startled to answer. It lightly crossed my mind that the two might have stopped by to see her on the way home. Then David popped out on the driver's side and said, "Is anything wrong with Mud, Mom? All the way up Barbara has been bugging me about Mud—worrying how she is!"

There have been other times when Barbara seemed to know about something that happened when she wasn't physically present. This capacity seems to have faded in

145

recent years, perhaps because her head has become filled with facts and figures of daily living, thus crowding out this fine "sixth sense" that we know so little about. I have wondered about the possibility that persons with so-called mental retardation might have more highly developed extrasensory perception than the rest of us. I have wanted to study at the respected Jung Institute in Zurich, where scholars have done impressive studies on ESP, but the uphill push for community programs here in California has had to come first.

We blundered and wondered a lot during the risk-taking teenage years of our three children. Of course, we worried about Barbara. We worried that someone might hurt her feelings, cheat her when she shopped, or take advantage of her trusting affection. But we also recognized that we cannot let our worry become her straitjacket. We must not cheat her of her right to failure, which is as integral a component of growth as is success.

I once heard the most damning indictment of parents uttered by a young woman with severe physical disabilities. "Disabled persons are the one oppressed minority," she said, "where the parents tend to be on the side of the oppressors."

I believe that parents need not fall into this category. We can become our sons' and daughters' allies and advocates in their striving for independence. This will not happen, however, until American society is willing to support its disabled members with fair and equal opportunities and support programs.

RESPONSIBILITY was an "all-cap" word in our household. It applied to daily school attendance, Sunday School, Scout meetings, and concerts. To Al and me a promise meant a total commitment, and we expected our children to abide by our standards of responsibility. In desperation David once turned to his father and burst out, "But what if I don't want to grow up to be as good as you, Dad!" With that we began to realize that a sense of responsibility must be learned and cannot be dictated. Everyone must experience the consequences of his or her own irresponsibility in order to opt for the opposite.

Of course, we were overwhelmingly concerned that Barbara learn responsible and appropriate behavior in the framework of our home, and gradually she did. She was clumsy and destructive at first. Favorite trucks lost wheels. Dolls were decapitated, and card games disappeared. It was difficult to act as referee between an irate older brother or sister, both of whom took care of their possessions, and Barbara, who was exploring with a vengeance. Later, she learned to leave their things alone, and although she occasionally still probes the innards of her transistor radio, she is generally better organized with her personal belongings than the rest of the family.

No secret formula aided this learning process. She was exposed to the same group dynamics as her brother and sister were. We praised and scolded, rewarded and punished, hugged and spanked. We learned that many concepts needed to be explained to Barbara with greater patience and repeated more often. We still catch her occasionally in giving flippant answers instead of telling the truth, and it is difficult for her to understand the difference between a white lie, which is socially acceptable and sometimes necessary, and a serious falsehood.

Becoming responsible involves many, many steps which are hard for anyone to take, and positive presumptions are needed to make it happen. Positive presumptions used to be whisked away from parents at the first mention of the big, bad words "mental retardation." Then, with the rug pulled out from under them, parents were scared into expecting failure, and their expectation would mushroom into a fear of almost everything else. We "over-handicapped" our children by definition.

Then we began to make decisions for our children. Had Al and I continued to decide for Barbara, she might never have learned to be responsible for any of her actions. Only by being presented with choices—be they ever so small and seemingly insignificant—can any child learn responsible behavior.

"Choice," according to Webster, is "the voluntary act of selecting or separating from two or more things that which is preferred." We let Barbara "select" when she came to restaurants with us (yes, we stared down the starers), and we encouraged her to order from a menu, though we had to read it to her. She would also go to the library and choose her own picture books and records.

There were unfortunate occasions, which I remember with embarrassment, when I was the one who put obstacles in the way of her "voluntary act of selecting that which is preferred." When Barbara announced that she wanted to grow her hair long like Karen's, I told her, "No! You look very nice with short hair, and it's a lot of work to take care of it when it's long. You have to rinse it a whole lot more when you wash it, and you'd have a hard time putting it up in curlers. No! Wait until you get bigger." As far as I was concerned, the subject was closed, but our girl persisted. As soon as Karen heard of the fuss, she went to bat for Barbara. "Why not, Mother? Why shouldn't she? Everybody is wearing their hair long these days." I gave in reluctantly, and for several years Barbara wore her hair long and managed to take care of it.

Another time we were shopping for a new outfit. Barbara tried on several slacks and tops, and we had narrowed down the choice to some grey flannel pants with a matching sweater and a dark red pantsuit which was identical with a bright green one she had chosen the year before. She looked pretty in either outfit, but I thought it was boring to have two suits just alike and said so. In fact, I really tried to talk her into the slacks and sweater. "But I like the red one," she said, "and it feels comfortable." With that we bought the one she preferred.

To learn to let her choose clothes and food was relatively easy and painless. Other choices were more difficult, and often I completely missed the cues she gave me. I blushingly remember one such incident when Barbara's tenth birthday was approaching. She and I were making a list of friends to invite to her party, and she wanted to ask just about everyone in her class and Susan, too. Susan was the little neighbor girl with whom she had gone to nursery school for a year. Now Barbara was at Paul Bunyan while Susan was attending elementary school. Susan had come to all of Barbara's previous parties, but for some reason I thought that she might have outgrown Barbara and her friends so I talked Barb out of asking Susan.

It was Susan's mother who set me straight. "Didn't Barbara have a birthday the other day?" she asked me when we met in town, "and didn't she have a party this year?" I explained that I had persuaded Barbara not to invite her friend because I had been afraid that Susan might not want to come. "You shouldn't have done that," she said. "Susan really cares about Barbara." Thoughtlessly, I had overridden one of Barbara's decisions. Because I was afraid of a potentially uncomfortable situation

149

for our girl, I came close to depriving her of the privilege of choosing a friend. Barbara knew that Susan liked her, but I had not listened. We soon mended that fence, and she and Susan enjoy each other to this day.

Readiness for role changes is the sixth and possibly the most difficult *R* to attain. The ups and downs of childishness and maturity are strangely unpredictable. The transition from childhood and dependence to adulthood and independence rarely happens smoothly. Yesterday our children piled into bed with us to snuggle. Today they pull away from hugs and kisses. Small bids for adult status may alternate with regressions into childish behavior, but overall, most children dream of becoming grown-ups and children with special needs are no different.

Barbara longed for the status symbol of female maturity, her monthly period, when she was only eleven. She could hardly wait to be old enough for SSI (Supplemental Security Income) benefits so that she would have her own money. The acquisition of a nondriver identification card from the Department of Motor Vehicles, complete with photo, was a source of tremendous pride to her. With Karen and David we had expected adulthood, but with Barbara it took jolt after small jolt to shake us out of our overprotective parental attitude.

One day Barbara complained of a little headache. "Want to take an aspirin?" I asked.

"I already did," she replied, and with that I jumped all over her. "Don't you remember," I roared, "that we have a rule in this house that you never take any medicine without asking?"

Her lower lip drooped. "But I know aspirin," and she quickly led me to the medicine cabinet and showed me the bottle. The thought suddenly occurred to me that our daughter was eighteen and a young adult. We were thinking of letting her move into a group home, and I couldn't unlearn my "smother" role. I apologized to Barbara. "We have a new rule now—a rule for young adults who know aspirin."

Another time, during her teenage years, Al and I assumed that she would go to a community concert with us. "I'm not going," she declared that evening. "Oh yes, you are! We've got season tickets, and we always go." I was afraid to leave her home alone for the evening, although we felt quite safe on our country road. We had a dog who was protective of her, and she could always phone in an emergency. Even so, I cajoled and pressured her a little longer. Finally she burst out in exasperation, "I hate that kind of music and I want my peace!" With this outburst she overcame our apprehension, and she accomplished her small bid for independence by a very elementary bit of communication. She asked for a quiet evening at home, and for a change we listened.

There is, of course, one ultimate role change which we all find difficult to contemplate, and that is death. I wonder if we do not tend to shield our children, especially those who have disabilities, from experiencing the grimmer side of life.

Barbara has worried about death and asked about it often. Death has already touched her life several times, and she will probably continue to question this inevitable reality. We have lost grandparents, a close young friend, and a good neighbor. Beloved dogs have met with sudden accidents. Again and again Barbara has asked, "Where is Nana now? What is Jack doing?" Each time we have tried to lead her towards accepting the fact that death comes to us all, and it will come to her, too.

151

"We all die, Barb," I would say. "Every day there are babies born all over the world, and old people die."

"Not me!" She'd shake her head. "I'm not going to," and with that turned off the conversation.

Barbara is twenty-six now. She has been living away from home for several years, and some of her friends have lost their mothers or fathers. "What is going to happen to me when you die?" she exploded like a bomb over breakfast on a recent weekend at home. "And who's going to live in our house?" She had never said "when" before, and never had she brought up the question of the house in which we have lived ever since she can remember. It seemed that she had taken a tremendous step towards acknowledging death as an inevitable part of the human condition.

It is rough going when someone is not prepared. Recently, a woman in a group home for adults with mental retardation lost her elderly father. A new staff person who asked the resident nurse for advice was told to give her a tranquilizer. What a repressive, unfeeling way of coping with pain! What a blatant denial of that young woman's humanity it was to buffer her grief with a pill! How can we prepare young people with special needs for the unavoidable dark side of our lives—sickness and death?

The process can begin in small steps and at an early age. Barbara inadvertently experienced a day and a night in the hospital when she was only a little girl. I was taking her temperature one day when she bit down too hard on the thermometer. It broke, and although I rescued both ends of it, I couldn't be 100 percent sure that she had not swallowed a bit of mercury. "Bring her down!" said our doctor, and after pumping out her stomach, he suggested that Barbara spend a day in the hospital.

"I'm almost certain that she's okay, but wouldn't this be a fine occasion to introduce her to a hospital experience?"

I nodded yes.

"How would you like to stay with us until tomorrow, Barbara? Just to make sure your tummy is all right?"

Barbara beamed from ear to ear. "Stay overnight?" And then, "Pack me a suitcase, Mom."

She knew exactly what she wanted in it, too! She lay in the six-bed ward like the Queen of the May and enjoyed all the friendly service. The nurses commented that she was such a good girl, and so cooperative. When we picked her up the following morning, she cried a little.

I remembered this happy happening a couple of years later, when a friend of mine was teaching a course for licensed vocational nurses. We agreed that all of my students ought to be prepared for a possible hospital stay, and her nursing students would also benefit from getting to know the children in our Paul Bunyan School. We introduced the children to hospital beds, bedpans, urinals, emesis basins, and hypodermic needles. The nursing instructor even volunteered to have an injection of distilled water. As she pulled the needle out of her arm, I heard one of our youngsters say, "Hey! You didn't even cry!" They were learning that shots really don't hurt that much.

When Barbara turned twelve, the age at which most hospitals permit children to visit patients, we began taking her along with us to see sick friends. She learned not to be afraid of our friend Jack's seizures. The first time he had one at our house, Barbara bluntly asked him to leave. "Go away!" she said. "Go to your house." She was acting out of fear rather than rudeness. As we talked with her, she learned to accept Jack's condition. Later, when he was hospitalized and slowly dying from a brain tumor, Barbara knew it. She vacillated between fear of seeing him close to death and wanting to visit him because she loved him. When she came along with us, he made her smile with his brave humor. "Jack isn't sad," she commented.

Whenever Barbara has experienced the loss of an anchor person in her life, we have tried to help her face her grief squarely. It has been difficult to explain death and life after death. Although we celebrate most traditional church holidays, we are not a formally religious family, and so heaven, hell, and resurrection are concepts that we have steered away from. We do remember and often talk about those who are gone now. We have tried to explain to Barbara that bodies decompose in graves or turn to ashes when cremated.

"And then the memories of the person who is dead live in our minds—in our head," I have said. "I remember my parents way back when I was a little girl, Barbara. Some memories are sad—when they were angry or spanked me—but mostly I remember happy things about them, and that's the way it's going to be for you, too, we hope. And you will have your brother and sister and counselor and many, many friends to be close to you and care about you."

We have held this dialogue not once but several times. I'm sure it hurts both of us each time, like growing pains, and I expect that she will continue to ask out loud as long as she questions death in her heart.

Just about a year ago, we went through it again, this time with our young friend, Linda Warner, who works as a social worker counselor on behalf of students with physical disabilities.

"Why don't you be my mother, Linda, when she dies?"

Barbara asked as she pointed in my direction.

"I can't be your mother," Linda answered honestly, "but I can be your friend and I want to be."

"And Karen and David will be your guardians," I began, but Barbara interrupted me in midsentence.

"Why don't you do it and get it over with!" she blurted out and left Linda and me speechless.

So we are trying to help her build bridges from the past to the present to an uncertain future. With her question, "What will happen to me when you die?" she seems to have established a first wobbly bridgehead to that scary future place.

In some small ways she seems to be able to handle death with more equanimity than I. A few months ago a neighbor phoned to tell me that she thought one of our cats had been run over and was lying on the road. I went to pick it up. It looked pretty messy, so I carried it gingerly by its tail and put it down just inside our driveway for Al to bury later. Barbara was home and cried just a little when I told her. Then she went out to see for herself, and when I looked out of the window, I was amazed to see her less afraid of handling the cat than I had been. She cradled it gently in her arms and talked to it softly. First she put it down in one place, and then another, until she found a soft, grassy spot close to the house. She came inside, washed her hands, and said, "That's better. This evening Al bury her."

It was a step forward from the time, several years ago, when our beloved dachshund, Wally, had been hit by a car and died during the night. We all got dressed that morning and were ready to go out with Al for Wally's burial. Except Barbara. She was still poking around in her bathrobe, looking sad.

"Come on, Barb, don't you want to come out and help Daddy bury Wally?" we urged her.

She shook her head.

"Why not? What do you want to do?"

"Can't we make a rug out of Wally?" was her wistful reply.

So Barbara is groping her way towards acceptance of death, and we're trying to help her as best we can. Recently, I met a gentleman who had just become a member of our regional center's board of trustees. I was introduced to him with the statement, "Mrs. Moise has a daughter with mental retardation." I shook his hand and welcomed him. "How'd you do," he said and added, "Sometimes I wish I were retarded, too. They're always so happy!" I recovered in time to tell that man that he was underestimating our sons and daughters and that they are people who know the full range of human emotions.

Later, I asked myself if we actually do let our children experience the full range of emotions. How can we honestly interpret their total humanness to others, if we, their parents, are less than honest with them? And honesty includes our preparing them for sickness and dying. They deserve no less than this.

I realize, of course, that Barbara has been blessed by the combined circumstances of a cohesive family and the supportive environment of a friendly small town. Not all families are as lucky as we are. We have been well endowed with health, energy, community support, and a steady income. And there are families who, in spite of similar supports, still cannot rise to the challenge of a child with special needs. Do we label them "failures" and categorically relegate their children to institutions or community group homes because they cannot cope?

Perhaps these parents' unwillingness to let their child off the "short leash" of dependence is caused by a deep-seated reluctance to say the word "Help!" Perhaps they perpetuate their disabled son or daughter in an eternal child role because of a very private need of their own, a hurt too raw to share. With intensified counseling by both professionals and fellow parents, they may be able to make a go of it. Given specific supports like respite care, homemaker services, and early developmental programs, their energies and coping skills may be released, so that their house may become a home for their child.

It is quite clear that not every family will cope in the same manner or with the same degree of success. American tradition is one of rugged individualism. This may have been more fitting for our pioneer forebears than it is for our complex twentieth-century society, but it still holds. People feel that they have the right to raise their kids the way they want. In some countries of the world children are registered at birth, and if they are found to be at risk for a disabling condition, they are followed along from the start, treated as necessary, and automatically provided habilitative programs by their government. In Austria, for example, a mother-child passport is issued to the mother at the first prenatal examination. It represents a commitment for her to follow through with all prenatal and postnatal examinations for herself and her baby well beyond the first year of life into childhood. As an inducement, there is a sizeable cash payment for fulfillment of all required check-ups. The system establishes good health and prevention habits for families, gives the Austrian health department a tremendous data base for the study of child health, and has placed Austria well ahead of the United States in infant mortality statistics.

Since Americans tend to bristle and balk at government interference in family life, we parents of children with developmental special needs must continue to assist one another. We must help the public to understand disabilities and the need for home support services. When these services become generally available to shore up families who are in need of support, all our children will be able to live "in the middle of things," as Bob Perske says, right in their hometowns where they belong.

11 *Farewell To Childhood*

ONE DAY WHEN ELEANOR MELVILLE, a close friend of our family, took Barbara to the store, she ran right into the need for a basic lesson in the facts of life. They wheeled their purchases to the check-out counter, and in the line in back of them was a man with a big pot belly hanging way out over his pants. Eleanor noticed Barbara's eyes riveted on the man's stomach. She could feel the question brewing, and out it came: "Are you going to have a baby?"

The checker sputtered with laughter. The fat man took it good-naturedly, and Eleanor explained that babies grow only in women's stomachs. She told me about the incident when I came to pick up Barbara, and though we didn't dwell on it then, it went down as one of the many markers on the road towards recognizing my child's sexuality and rightful need for information.

My fears about her womanhood stemmed from the time when she was a year and a half old, and we had first received the diagnosis of mental retardation. I asked our close friend and family physician, "What will happen when Barbara matures, Lloyd? Will men take advantage of her? Do you think she'll ever be able to marry and have children?" This kind and thoughtful man tried to set my mind at ease by saying, "You've got a lot of time, Lotte, and in your home I can see no reason why she should not be able to learn the difference between right and wrong."

It was an old-fashioned answer. Almost a nonanswer to an impossible question. As gently as he could, Lloyd shifted the burden of responsibility onto our family's shoulders. Right then I made up my mind that sex would have no place in Barbara's life. Just how I expected to accomplish this, however, was still unclear. I had too many other concerns that were more pressing. The fact that I did was fortunate, for I had time to observe and think—and change.

The changes did not take place in any logical, lock-step sequence. First I had to work through my own experiences and come to grips with the differences in Al's and my sexual attitudes. By the time Barbara reached physical maturity, he and I had already become our children's teachers and models—for better or for worse!

Al's and my attitudes and taboos are distinctly different. My Europe-based feelings towards sexuality are a little more open and perhaps less puritanical than his American views. Certainly my physician father, who specialized in venereal diseases, helped me.

I remember asking Papi about premarital relationships when I was in my teens. His advice went something like this: "I really think that up to the age of about twenty-one, a girl is better off not experimenting with sex, because it can get her into sticky situations both physically and emotionally. But, if you haven't found a desirable marriage partner when you are in your mid-twenties, I'd certainly advise you to have an affair, because I would not want you to miss out on this very wonderful dimension in life. And if you're ever in any kind of difficulty—remember—you can always come home!"

Pretty progressive and reassuring advice for a father to give to his daughter forty-five years ago! Mother would cluck and admit that when she was a girl, she wasn't able to get answers to the specific kind of questions that I was asking my dad.

Even so, I was much too scared—scared of venereal disease, pregnancy, and social ostracism—to have acted on his advice. I was a virgin at age twenty-eight when I met my future husband. We had a glorious premarital honeymoon traveling up the Alaska Highway together in our jeep and were married a short time later. I remember that we were a little worried about how we might explain this slightly unusual sequence of events to our children, but it took care of itself. An elderly aunt of my husband's commented, "That must have been an interesting trip you and Alfred took together. If I hadn't known that my nephew is such a gentleman, I might have had second thoughts about it!"

My two years in the Coast Guard during World War II certainly broadened my outlook on life. There I found out that my own social and sexual views marked just one spot on a continuum. Some young women were a lot more conservative than I, while others were more enterprising in their sexual activities. I learned to like and respect one girl who was striking it rich, entertaining sailors in her apartment in town, and she was one of the best workers on the base. I could always count on Kelly to be on time and efficient, and long after our discharge, when I was back in a New York office working from nine to five, she was still sending me glorious full-color postcards from Hawaii. For the first time I encountered women who were Lesbians, and I was involved in counseling with one SPAR who had resorted to an illegal abortion while another single woman

161

I knew would not think of having her pregnancy terminated. (In the service both homosexuality and illegal abortions were offenses which could result in prison terms.) I began to realize that my own position on sexual matters was as uniquely mine as my fingerprints.

Substitute teaching in the Fort Bragg schools in the early fifties also influenced my thinking. Several times I happened into the all girls' class in family life education—sex education of a sort. Invariably the students asked, "Why are they teaching us this stuff now? We needed it when we were in the fifth or sixth grade!" Occasionally I bumbled into boys' biology just as their textbook discussed female menstruation. I had no advance warning but decided that there was no cause for panic. After all, these were just nice little boys like the one I had at home (which ain't so, because high school kids tend to be brats when they have a substitute!). I waded right into the subject on the assumption that they all had mothers or sisters at home and would be having girl friends, wives, and daughters in due time. I introduced the topic by saying that menstruation is a natural process and that they had better stop being silly and learn about it. It went okay. My increasing ability to talk about matters of sexual functioning in a relaxed manner was a great step forward.

Although Al's family background was more restrained than mine, he came into wedlock with lots more swinging experience. He had chased a series of girls up and down the Santa Monica Canyon in a series of hopped-up cars while I was still a good little German schoolgirl. He had lost one wife and divorced another, and we were both determined to make this marriage work. Yet, when I think back now, our premarital discussions seem surprisingly naive. We certainly didn't have the vaguest premonition of what Gail Sheehy, author of *Passages,* calls "predictable crises of adult life!" We learned by trial and error.

Our first arguments about sexuality took place when the children were still quite small. Al has an earthy, corny sense of humor, which is irrepressible. He loves puns and limericks, and the mere hint of anything sexual brings out the best (or worst!) in him. At suppertime he would spontaneously burst out with jokes. "Al! Please! Not in front of the children!" I'd protest. He could not understand that I wanted to keep the subject innocent and ideal for them. I took sex seriously and did not learn about its lighthearted aspects until later.

Trying to stay one step ahead of our children in their social/sexual learning process accustomed me to sudden, startling questions. They rarely waited for an appropriate time or place. There was never any time for parental consultation. They wanted to know now, and if the answer didn't fit, they went on to something else. Sometimes they weren't ready for a technical answer and asked the same question again later. One friend of mine settled down to give her young adolescent son a well-prepared, serious explanation of intercourse and was totally undone because he laughed merrily. She never did find out what struck him funny. She was so upset that she vowed to make her husband take his turn with their other boys.

Basically, I gave our children the same sort of information that I had received from my parents. Both Al and I tried to help them understand that the subject of sex is not a secret, but that it is a personal part of their lives.

Barbara needed specific, frequent explanations of certain simple ground rules which David and Karen had picked up on their own. Not long after she had wondered about the fat man's belly, we were downtown on a fine

sunny day, watching a parade. A convertible zipped by
with the top down, and the guy driving it was bare
chested. "Ooh!" yelled Barbara. "He's all naked."

"Oh no he's not," I said. "He only took his shirt off, and
it's okay for boys to take their tops off."

"But it's not okay for girls to take their tops off," added
David anxiously.

"So, you see, Barb," I continued, "he's not naked
because he's a boy and he only took his shirt off." And as I
said this, I caught my young son's eye and we burst out
laughing. We had both heard the inanity of our dialogue,
and yet it was important for Barbara to learn this particular nuance of where one can do what and when.

Luckily, she was the youngest of three, so Al and I had
an idea of what to expect in children's behavior, and
Karen and David automatically helped with the process of
educating their young sister. "No, Barbara! You can't
come out like that. Put your nightgown on!" one of them
would yell as she toddled out into the living room naked,
and they'd wheel her around and push her back into the
bedroom. Or they'd shout at her to close the bathroom
door behind her. Such small object lessons in appropriate
social behavior have to precede more advanced knowledge in sexual morals and mores. In spite of this, she
often embarrassed me when she was a little girl. She'd
walk up behind unsuspecting gentlemen who were peace-
fully reading in the library, and gave them big hugs. I
could not explain to them that this pretty little girl felt
warmly towards the world and had not yet learned to
channel this feeling appropriately. At times it is still difficult for her to shake the hand of an attractive young man
whom she has just met, when she feels the urge to show
affection, and then I worry about her.

Three years ago when we were on a brief return visit to Copenhagen, Barbara and I landed in separate seats in the same streetcar. There is something about her robust, rosy appearance that seems to appeal to Danish men. I had noticed this before, so I wasn't too surprised to see a young man sit down beside her. He began to talk to her—first in Danish, then English. He came on strong, obviously trying to pick her up, and at first Barbara looked pleased. But when he tried to put his arm around her, she became uncomfortable and glanced over to me as if she expected me to intercede. Finally, just as we were getting to our stop, she pointed to me and shouted in his ear, "That's my mom, Lotte!"

She still has a lot to learn, and so have we all.

It was our Danish experience of 1971 that initially started the wheels turning in my head. We realized, of course, that the Danes have a realistic, relaxed attitude towards relationships between men and women, those with mental retardation naturally included. While Barbara spent the month living in the Copenhagen group home, it was a residence for young women only, but boyfriends were very much a part of the everyday scenery.

Discussions of each resident's problems with relationships, dating, marriage, and child rearing were tackled as they came up. Either Elna Skov, the director, or one of her well-trained care assistants would sit down with the young woman, and sometimes her boyfriend, and they would discuss matters of physiology and contraception. There were no specially prepared textbooks then. Elna used an old book of home nursing advice, which was richly illustrated, and began her instruction wherever the individual happened to be. "The majority of our girls don't know much when they come here from the institution or from their own families. So I try to find out what they know and go from there. And when they tell me, 'My boyfriend is afraid to use a condom,' for whatever reason, then I know that it's time to invite him to sit in on our lessons."

Barbara really didn't live in the group home long enough to become involved in dating activities, and without an outside work assignment she had little opportunity to meet young men. Surprisingly, the language barrier turned out not to be a barrier at all, and the reason may have been that Barbara had become used to communicating across her speech handicap. At any rate she managed well. She felt free to visit the other young women in their rooms and worked along happily in the kitchen with a housekeeper who didn't speak a word of English! So she, too, could have had a boyfriend.

On her evaluation report the staff persons noted: "Barbara gets along well with peers and friends—does not seem to need more social contact—but wants sexual contact badly."

I came home with my mother's heart in a state of palpitation. Conflicting thoughts and feelings tossed and turned, especially in the area of sexuality. I was trying to come to grips with my parental fears for Barbara and to examine my own ambivalent attitudes on such loaded issues as masturbation, premarital sex, birth control, homosexuality, and abortion.

I was certainly not alone in my quest for answers. Others were reaching the same point of concern. A workshop on the subject of sexuality resulted. The pediatrician who organized the event, invited a parent (me) and a special education teacher along with some of his students to take part in the discussions. First thing in the morning the good doctor drew some charts and graphs on the blackboard, which illustrated the incidence of mental retardation in children born to mothers with the same disability. It was high compared with national norms. For me, this was a discouraging beginning, unsubstantiated as it was by comparable figures of mothers who, though developmentally delayed, might have passed into the so-called normal population. I felt scared rather than reassured, and I was reminded that much of today's knowledge of mental retardation is still rooted in the eugenics movement of the early twentieth century, which had people believing that those whom they called idiots and imbeciles would outbreed us all.

The students, thank goodness, did not join us until afternoon. They were a bunch of nervous, giggly teenage boys and girls who fielded personal questions about their social needs and desires thrown at them by a group of strangers. They all attended a school in the country, and most of them lived on ranches and helped with the care of animals and other chores. One pretty girl with Down's syndrome was able to express some of her frustration at having to go everywhere with her mom and dad while her brothers and sisters took off on their own because they could drive. The students appeared totally inexperienced in the realm of adolescent feelings and relationships.

After they left the room, the discussion ranged widely. Someone made the point that they might remain innocently childlike and sexually unaware. This was challenged by a group home worker who thought that there was need for social training and instruction in sexuality. One father anxiously and repeatedly said, "Our Jim has never even thought about sex or gone near a girl. He kisses his mother goodnight—that's all. Leave him alone! You'll only stir him up!"

167

I couldn't believe that it was worse to "stir up" feelings of closeness and affection that are real, than to bury them by evasion. I thought of the many clues and signals that our children—Barbara as well as the others—had given of their social and sexual maturing.

All three children routinely bounced into our beds to snuggle in the mornings. Imperceptibly this tapered off during Karen's and David's adolescence. If we thought about it at all, we must have assumed that they were establishing contact with someone of the opposite sex, at least in their imagination. But what about Barbara? What was she to do with her need for warmth and touching? What would take the place of snuggling in bed with her parents when this no longer seemed appropriate or possible?

We noticed that she was masturbating. She'd sit in a comfortable armchair in the living room, rub her thighs together, and jiggle with pleasure. By then we had learned that masturbation was not harmful, contrary to the messages of our own childhood. Even in a family as medically sophisticated as mine, there seemed to have been reluctance to permit children to stimulate their bodies. I vaguely recalled a bedtime scene when Papi brought Aunt Martha, a pediatrician, to my bedroom for our goodnight ritual. I was almost asleep, snuggled under the covers, when they lowered their voices to a whisper. With my rabbit ears I thought I heard something about not permitting me to keep my hands under the covers. Even though I was not quite sure what I heard, I pulled my arms out to give them both hugs. I wondered about it later and learned to keep my masturbating activities strictly private.

In Barbara's case we said repeatedly and firmly: "Not here! Not in the living room, Barbara. We know it feels good to jiggle, but it belongs in the privacy of your bed-room or bathroom. You've learned to go wee-wee in the bathroom. You must learn this, too."

David recently admitted that he had some unanswered questions about masturbation when he was a kid. "I never saw you do it," I said in surprise, "and Dad and I simply assumed that you knew it was okay, son!"

"Yeah! but I got plenty of conflicting messages from the community," he said. "It would have helped if you'd brought up the subject. Remember the time Sam and I went camping? How'd ya think we got poison oak on our genitals?"

The fact that old wives' tales about masturbation still abound in this day and age is scarily real. A couple of years ago I was invited to talk to a parent group about social and family life education for their adult children. I took along the British film *Like Other People,* in which young people with cerebral palsy touchingly and eloquently discuss their feelings about relationships and love. There was silence when I first turned off the projector. I had expected this. It was a group of elderly parents in a small, "straight" logging and fishing community, who might find it difficult to talk about something so personal. In the back of the room I had noticed a younger couple, and the man spoke up first. He had liked the film very much. The feelings expressed in it were "right on." He managed to get the discussion rolling, for which I was grateful.

Then he came to the front and said hesitantly, "There was something I wanted to ask, but I didn't want to ask it in front of the others. Is it true that masterbating can cause brain damage? That's what my mother told me. She said it's the cause for my being slow."

"No!" I said. "But there are many others of our genera-

169

tion who were told the same thing by their mothers and fathers."

He smiled and thanked me. Then he turned back to the young woman who was standing next to him. He put his arm lightly on her shoulder and said, "Of course, now that I have a woman, I don't need it any more!"

Barbara matured physically earlier than either Karen or I. She was only eleven when she yelled to me from the bathroom one day, "Mummy, Mummy, come quick!" When I rushed to see what had happened, she was beaming. "Look! I got my period!"

She was probably not able to understand all the intricacies of female plumbing which caused the flow of blood, but she knew that it happened every month and that we bathed routinely and wore a pad or tampon. Karen and I had made it a point to tell her about our menstrual periods and to show her matter of factly how we took care of them. Barbara was looking forward to the event as a status symbol of adulthood. Unfortunately, it turned out to be a false alarm. She had eaten a lot of fresh beets the night before!

When Barbara actually had her first period some time later, it was a terrible disappointment. Not only did it hurt, but it went on for days—almost two weeks. We finally had to consult our doctor, who prescribed small doses of birth control pills which regulated matters. She still grouches occasionally, but she has learned to accept menstrual periods as a respected part of the female condition.

Barbara established her right to privacy on the day after Bob Perske had spoken at our first major California conference on the sexuality of our children. He told of his swing around the Scandinavian countries and brought great news of educational and living arrangements for persons with developmental special needs. He discussed privacy in the Danish group homes which he had seen. Barbara was at the conference with us, but I didn't think that she had paid attention to anything that was being discussed. The next day I went barrelling into our bathroom while she was sitting on the toilet, and she yelled at me, "Stop! Knock first!" I reeled back with a red face, knocked, re-entered, and said, "Hey! You heard what Mr. Perske said yesterday, didn't you?" She smiled and nodded.

And remember the automatic prohibition against sex that I had vowed to uphold? Well, I had to reverse that when she was quite a young teenager. A student from our activity center was spending a weekend at our house while his parents were away. One day I saw the two of them sitting on the sofa hand in hand. He seemed a bit embarrassed, but Barbara beamed at him adoringly. Right then I knew that we could not possibly relegate all boy/girl relationships into never-never land for her. It would be cruel to keep this essential dimension of life from her.

We were lucky to have had Karen and David first, for they readied us for the funny misunderstandings and confusions of all children as they ask and learn about sex. Barbara found it more difficult to ask questions, but we learned to look for cues. I could see question marks in her eyes and sense situations that were going to be socially difficult for her. Luckily, we lived in the country and were able to use animals as object lessons, or so we thought.

One evening when Al came home, he looked out the window to the field across the road and announced, "Hey! Mr. Gregg's horse got married, I hear, and soon she's going to have a baby." Sure enough five-year-old Karen wanted to know how horses got married, and Al threw me a despairing glance. I answered for him. "Well, children, Mr. Gregg took the mummy horse down the road to Mr. Junker who has a daddy horse, and the daddy horse put the seed inside the mummy horse's tummy, so now the baby is growing inside the mummy and will soon come out. Horses are different from people, though. They don't live in families quite like we do, so the mummy and the baby may not see the daddy very often."

Karen looked puzzled and said, "I don't understand, Mom. Horses don't dance, do they?"

It was my turn to be puzzled. "What do you mean, dear?"

"Well," said Karen, "I don't see how horses can marry if they can't dance at their wedding!"

The biology had obviously been wasted on her, but the story has a sequel. The foal was born and was galloping around the field about a year and a half later when David was about five. As I was keeping him company while he waited for the school bus one day, he wanted to know if the foal came out of the mummy horse's tummy and how it got there. I gave him verbatim the same answer as I had given to Karen, but when I mentioned Mr. Junker, David interrupted: "Mr. Junker? Why him? Why didn't Mr. Gregg take her to Mr. Windus?"

Since the Windusses didn't own a horse, I was stumped again. "Mr. Windus doesn't have a horse, does he, Dave?"

"Oh!" said David thoughtfully, "it has to be another horse!"

We accumulated a variety of pets over the years. Besides the standard number of country cats, there was always one dog. At one point Karen won a duck at a fair by tossing a dime into a dish. It grew up to be a mean beast who terrorized our favorite cat. Then there was a large turtle. Al drilled a hole through its shell so that Karen could take it for walks on a leash. We also raised a couple of lambs whose mothers were unable to take good care of twins, or "bummers," as they're called by the ranchers. Each time a lamb was ready to return to the ranch, its owner would repay us with a luscious leg of lamb, and we were faced with the problem of disguising the origin of the meat. "No, children, this is not our lamb," we would tell them.

Barbara had to take her turn with the responsibilities of caring for these pets as soon as she was able, and Karen and David saw to it that she did. "It's your turn!" was their stern command. Karen's mare, Chips, was too large for Barbara to handle, but she did sit on her and walked around the yard several times. She also took part in the joys of Chip's and Karen's minor triumphs of horsemanship.

Dogs were our main pets, and we had a rule that they should always be boy dogs. We didn't want the additional work of raising puppies and turned down several offers of cute female dogs who happened to need a good home. Well, one time we were had! A shaggy little mutt kept coming around to visit and to eat. He/she looked like nothing at all and wouldn't stand still for closer inspection. Neighbors down the road assured us that it was a male and had been deliberately dropped off from a passing car. The children named it Prince and begged us to keep it, but Al and I refused. The matter was just about settled when in Karen came dragging Barbara by the hand. "You can't give that dog away now, Dad. It's 'Princess,' not 'Prince.' She and George just got married. Barbara and I saw it!"

So Princess stayed and became one of ours. When she went into labor, there was tremendous excitement and Al even came home from work early. She gave birth right under the kitchen window, and Barbara could see each of the five little sacks as they came out and were licked clean into wiggly little pups. Just the other day she reminded me of the event. (Again we have broken our own rule and have a female dog who is expecting!) "Remember Princess?" she said. "Call me when the puppies come out so I can see them."

Such live demonstrations are really worth a thousand words, for most children with developmental special needs remain insulated from real information. Most have difficulties in asking questions, and the words in books remain a blank. Rarely can they sneak a look at porny periodicals like other children do, and TV is more erotically stimulating than specifically informative. It tends to add to the confusion of the already mixed-up morals and mores of our culture. Unfortunately, special education classes have steered away from family life education until quite recently.

When I first worked as a counselor at a summer camp for young adults back in 1960, we were told in our counselor indoctrination, "Now this is a bit like a resort, and there may be some infatuations. If you see a boy and girl walking down the trail with their arms around each other or holding hands, we suggest that you just quietly walk between them, put your arms on their shoulders, and say something like 'Hey, isn't it a nice day!' "

I have to admit that Al and I were caught up in the fear of those early days. We, too, became frightened. At the time Barbara was entering adolesence, we heard that a young woman in a nearby town's sheltered workshop had become pregnant. We were told that this young woman came from a problem home and that she was poorly supervised. She had a history of acting out sexually, and she was much less socially responsible than our own daughter. And yet we panicked. We could not seem to square our new-found awareness of Barbara's need for warmth and friendship with our concern for her safety and well-being. We sought advice from a physician and arranged for her to have a tubal ligation. Barbara trusted this doctor, and she trusted us. We all hid behind his advice to her that she needed to have her appendix removed, and she and I did not talk about the primary purpose of the surgery until much, much later. Even then, as the day of the surgery came closer, Al and I began to feel the weight of our action. We were aware that we were manipulating a human being. Now I know that we should have waited. Barbara should have been told of this decision, which affected one of the basic functions of her body. She understood more than we gave her credit for, and later she was able to express to me her sense of loss and deprivation.

I do not think that Barbara could ever be fully responsible for the care of a child. I certainly would not want her to become pregnant either accidentally or otherwise. I have little faith in the efficiency or health benefits of current methods of birth control for women. Thus a tubal ligation might still have been the simplest and best way for our daughter, but it should and could have waited a few more years so that we could have discussed it with her honestly.

A Danish mother recently wrote "A Letter to Kirsten— but also to Parents" on the eve of her daughter's sterilization operation. She says that her girl is nineteen, pretty, and well able to take care of her daily living needs, but she

175

is somewhat handicapped by cerebral palsy. It is an agonizing letter which concludes as follows:

> I, your mother, have explained to you all the disadvantages of a pregnancy, have told you about the heavy responsibility of bringing a child into the world, told you what a burden it would be for your health, for your future, for your independence—and I have done this based on what I believe and believe very deeply and after many struggles—is best for you. And at the same time I feel guilty.
>
> There has been a lot of consultation. All kinds of papers have gone back and forth. Some people have talked with you and some with both of us— and tomorrow—you will be the same girl, lively and dear, but without the ability to bear a child.
>
> That will be tomorrow—another day—another Kirsten. I wonder if I took time enough, words enough to tell you about the joys of being a mother.

I feel with this mother more deeply than I can say.

It was at least three years later that Barbara first spoke of the tubal ligation. She was having her period and complaining about cramps. I was giving mildly consoling advice when she burst out, "Why didn't you take it all out?"

I was astounded. She had obviously found out about the consequences of the operation while I hadn't had the guts to talk to her about it. She must have also heard from other young women who had both their ovaries and uterus removed that this eliminated having periods.

I spoke with Barbara as frankly as I could. I told her why we thought that she'd be better off not having babies, but

that I'm truly sorry now that we did not tell her about it before the operation. I tried to assure her that it's okay to be
a woman without a baby, like her Aunt Grace. I can't
remember exactly what she said because the pain of it all
has blurred my memory, but I know that she somehow
conveyed to me that she felt cheated and sad. Occasionally she has spoken about it again. And she loves babies.

In some ways Barbara benefited by her brother's and
sister's late blooming adolescence, and it gave us all time
to catch up with one another's changing attitudes. For
many years I was more concerned about the social progress of our two older ones than I was about their sexual precocity. They were both comparatively short and
chubby—definitely not "in" with the popular kids—and
while Karen agonized about her lack of popularity, I was
secretly relieved that I did not have to face the heavy
problems of coping with a sexually active teenager. It was
not until they returned from college with their friends and
openly challenged our ground rules about boys sleeping in
the boys' room and girls in the girls' room that we began to
have differences of opinion. Al and I argued bitterly with
them about the appropriateness of these sleeping arrangements under our roof and about respect for our
values. They called us up-tight and hypocritical. Karen
won the last round in these debates. "Do you want to
know me as I really am, Mother?" she challenged one day,
"or shall I fake?" With that we began a more mature, adult
relationship, in which we were able to respect and accept
each other's differing values.

We found their honesty admirable. Their accusations
of hypocrisy hit home. We needed some of this same
gutsiness with which they stood up to us in order to
defend Barbara's right to be a sexual human being. We

177

also needed it to combat our own worries as she occasionally ventured forth into their free-wheeling world.

Her social and sexual learnings have not all been
smooth sailing. She was eighteen when she moved away
from home for real. She had wanted to live in Marin
County ever since Gary Hermes, who had worked with our
young adults on the coast, had moved there to direct a
work activity center. We arranged for her school placement and then started looking for a suitable place for her
to live. Even as late as 1972, in this sophisticated Bay Area
community, it was like pulling hen's teeth. I could never
have accomplished it without the assistance of a fellow
mother, Emmy Sokoloff, who had years of experience of
advocating for her own daughter. Barbara moved into a
shiny new home with a woman who was just getting her license as a caretaker and who had well-documented experience as staff person in another group home. All went well
at first. Barbara's weekend reports about school were
glowing and those about the home slightly more guarded.
Once or twice she spoke of the housemother's drinking
too much, but we thought it was Barbara's immature way
of getting back at the authority figure who was making her
toe the line and do her chores. After due deliberation,
however, we did decide to confront the woman with
Barbara's allegation as tactfully as possible. She assured
us that all was under control.

That summer Barbara spent a long, happy vacation
with us at home, and she was full of enthusiasm when she
moved back at the beginning of school. The housemother
looked hale and hearty, trimmer from losing twenty
pounds. We were at ease until the situation became
critical.

There was a drinking problem! One evening the woman

went out on a binge and brought her drunken boyfriend home. She herself passed out in the hall, and he molested our daughter. We have never been able to find out from Barbara exactly what happened, but we know that it was a traumatic sexual experience. Physically she was all right afterwards, but since then she has been very scared of pelvic examinations, which are routinely necessary for all young women. In spite of the encounter, she would like a boyfriend, although she may hope more for snuggly closeness and gentle expressions of love than sexual relations. That, too, may come to her in time.

We now realize that child raising takes one through an accelerating series of calculated risks which reach a crescendo during adolescence. We worry about our daughter's going out in a car with her boyfriend. We wonder what goes on when our son spends the proverbial weekend with a boyfriend. We want to trust, but we worry. We hope that they will learn.

Not so with youngsters with developmental special needs. We fight for them like tigers, but keep them in a protective pouch like kangaroos. They ride the little yellow school bus back and forth to special schools and work activity centers, stealthily holding hands. Then they return home and wait for the next special party—from Valentine's Day until Easter to the Fourth of July—and at those affairs they have about as much privacy as peas in a pod. Then, when they reach the magic age of legal adulthood, we expect them to have accomplished responsible adult behavior as if by some miracle.

This is where we parents come in as advocates for our sons and daughters while they are growing up. We must face the fact that it is ignorance, not information and knowledge, that breeds promiscuity and trouble. Social and sexual education must be real-life education, and real-life education begins when one is born and never ends. Real-life education must include real-life experiences, and that means personal relationships that start with one's family, widen to friends in school, friends at work, friends of the same sex, and then those of the opposite sex—each in their own sweet time of readiness. We must face the fact that responsibility and relationships do not develop in a vacuum. They can be and must be learned.

How we wish that Barbara could enjoy more of this essential human warmth. The occasions were few and far between during her teens, but memorable. One time, when she was home on vacation, our friends and co-workers, Brian and Marjorie Shears, came to visit us with their three children and Marjorie's brother, Stanley, who has Down's syndrome. Stanley lives in another state, and he was spending a few weeks with his sister. All beds were taken, so on the first night Stanley rolled out his brand-new sleeping bag and slept soundly on the living room rug. The next evening Barbara dragged out her sleeping bag and announced that she would sleep in the living room with Stanley and did so. After our friends had left, she confided to me with a radiant smile that she and Stanley had kissed before they went to sleep.

I think that it is our responsibility to provide such supportive learning experiences for our children, and that this puts a large advocacy responsibility on our shoulders.

I met a young social worker at a conference in another western state where we discussed family life education for young persons with developmental special needs. He told us of driving out to a farm to talk to the parents of one of his workshop students about their daughter's moving into a group home. He noticed a nicely framed photo of the young woman and her boyfriend on the mantel. The young man also attended the center and lived on a neighboring ranch.

The parents told the social worker of the two young people's long years of friendship and growing affection. Recently, they had begun to spend weekends at each other's home. When it seemed clear that they were able to cope by themselves, the parents arranged to take off for an occasional weekend, leaving the young couple alone and giving them a chance to test their relationship. Now they were planning to buy a trailer house for the two, so that they could begin to live with each other in an informal way. It blew the social worker's mind. He had come to talk to them patronizingly about permitting their daughter to move into a transitional independent living situation, and they were light years ahead of him! As he wound up his story, he blurted out, "I'm beginning to think that if it were possible for more of our people to get married, we wouldn't need so many social workers!"

He has a solid, valid point, and one that we ought to remember as our young people bid farewell to childhood. I also think it's time to ask those whom we label "mentally retarded" to tell us what they think they should learn before getting married. Young men and women in one of our premarital counseling courses drew up the following list of suggested learnings:

> Both husband and wife should have steady jobs first. You should get along with your roommate. No way can you make it with a girl if you can't get along with your roommate.
>
> One should have a thousand dollars in the bank.
>
> They should teach us how not to have babies.

The list of qualifications that these young people cite as prerequisites to marriage is impressive, and I have yet to see one like it posted in a church or judge's chambers where people are wed.

I'm glad that Barbara has learned to get along with others from an early age. Now that she is a young woman, we can watch her glow when a nice young man pays her some attention. It clearly boosts her self-esteem. She still has a way to go in learning how to make friends with someone she has just met without coming on too strong. She is making progress, though, and with her solid foundation in both casual and close relationships, she is now able to understand specific information about the physical facts of her body's functioning and the need for taking responsibility for her behavior. Way back during Paul Bunyan School days in the mid-sixties, when I was supervising the work training center for adults and Dodie Scott had become a teacher at the school, we decided that it was time to do a lesson on menstruation for her pupils. All we had as teaching aids were some free booklets from a sanitary napkin company. When I phoned Dodie to check on the results of this monumental lesson, she reported, "Not much happened. It was sorta disappointing. I think Barbara was more interested in the circus that's coming to town than in her body." We resigned ourselves to the fact that we would have to try another time.

Barbara came home brandishing the circus tickets, and that's all we talked about at first. Later that evening I thought I heard her say something about eggs. I wasn't sure I had heard right. "Dodie teach about eggs," she said. "Today—in school—my eggs, down here," and patted herself on the lower abdomen. So something had landed after all! Not much, but it was a beginning.

Her understanding is more sophisticated now. Two years ago Karen and a couple of fellow students decided to teach a short family life education course, as part of their family nurse practitioner training, to a group of Barbara's friends. They brought with them plastic models of the lower half of both men's and women's bodies with parts that they could not only see and touch, but remove and replace. She tells me that the course went well, and as an indirect result of it, Barbara has recently dared to insert a tampon for the first time in her life. To me all of this is further proof that clinical presentations of drawings, slides, and plastic models simply interest her in a factual way.

When Barbara was a child, we had many opportunities for mother-daughter talks. Now that she is an adult I am not always with her when she has a question or a problem. But I have a lot of faith in the many young teachers, counselors, and Planned Parenthood staffers, who have been trained in the special skills of family life education. And perhaps some of the essentials of sex education will make more of an impression when they are taught by someone outside of the home. After all, it sometimes takes a police officer, who comes to school in full uniform, to drive home the lesson of "Stop! Look! Listen!"

In time sex education may become an integral part of regular education, and then it will self-destruct. Most of it is plain common sense anyway, and whether we know it or not, we already teach it to our children daily. But since sexual relationships and attitudes towards them will always remain intensely personal, we parents expect teachers to respect our widely differing moral and religious beliefs. And, since our children will grow up to be adults, they should have an equal right to make informed choices. We hope that Barbara is acquiring sufficient knowledge to protect her from promiscuity, inappropriate behavior, and exploitation.

The main messages that I would like her and her friends to hear are the following:

> Sex and sexual activities are private.
>
> Sex is enjoyable, but the sex act produces babies unless we use birth control, and we don't want to put unwanted babies into the world.
>
> We must never touch another person's body against their will, nor should we let anybody touch us just to please them.

I think the change is gradually coming. *Like Other People,* a beautifully sensitive documentary film about the emotional needs of persons with disabilities, contains one particularly significant passage. A young man with severe cerebral palsy is asked, "Can retarded people experience love?" He replies, "Being retarded has nothing to do with love. They're capable of very deep love. Those who are intellectually able have more interests—more ways to substitute for love. If you're retarded you give your whole being to love."

More than anything else, Al and Karen and David and I wish Barbara a life that includes love.

12 *Update*

BARBARA'S LIFE SINCE 1971 has moved fast for a small town girl. Until then she had never been farther away from home than Disneyland! Our Danish experience launched us on a search for a dignified developmental lifestyle for our daughter here in our state. Again, she started the process. After eleven years of going to school in the same little old house on a quiet side street, with the same teacher and the same small group of fellow students day in and day out, she began to rebel. "I wanna go somewhere!" she complained as I shoved her onto the formerly beloved school bus. Once, in a wild moment of frustration, I asked her how she'd like to go back to Denmark to live. "They don't talk right," was her reply.

As a realistic solution to her restlessness, we enrolled her in Magnolia Park School in nearby Marin County. From a program for twelve children of all ages, she went to a co-educational school with fifty young adults. The school had prevocational programs. There was a shop equipped with power tools where students made wooden objects. They also learned how to take care of small animals and hired out as a crew to do gardening work. Some learned photography and simple duplicating. Barbara took particular pride in her ceramics, and she loved the choir and rhythm band. For the first time in her life our daughter had a chance to perform before a large group of parents and guests in the assembly program that concluded the school year.

Al and I had been invited, of course, and drove the hundred and fifty miles on a sunny Saturday afternoon to share in her joy. The auditorium was filled with about two hundred proud parents and friends. There were speeches by special educators and presentations of diplomas and special honors. Then came the entertainment—a series of songs accompanied by the rhythm band. Barbara was one of the singers. She had spotted us in the audience, and we could tell that her excitement mounted. This also increased the volume of her voice to a full crescendo. One of her more experienced schoolmates noticed the blast and gaver her a slight nudge in the ribs, whereupon our daughter turned around and gave her the finger in full view of the audience! It was spontaneous but totally inappropriate. She was bawled out for it, and I hope she has learned by now that obscene gestures get one into trouble!

Even the unhappily abrupt ending of her living arrangement while going to school did not discourage her. We all rallied around her to think through what to do next. Ann and Norm Hermstead, her teacher and principal, opened up their home to her for the first few crucial days, and then she came home for a week's vacation to relax and to recover. She said she wanted to stay at Magnolia Park School, and when Eva and Bill Bonge, the parents of a school friend, offered their home for the rest of the school year, she accepted happily. We reorganized all of Barbara's worldly belongings, and she returned to Marin County.

Many good things happened for Barbara during that

year. Mrs. Bonge put her on a strict diet, and she slimmed down to a glamorous weight and size. The loss of weight combined with a good exercise program improved her mobility. Al and I noticed how much more clearly she was enunciating words and found out that a speech therapist had been working with her at school. We all hoped that she would be able to stay at Magnolia Park two more years, until the legal age limit of twenty-one, but that was impossible without a place for her to live. The Bonges' daughter graduated that year, and they, too, were looking for an out-of-home living arrangement.

It was the summer of 1973. California's network of regional counseling and diagnostic centers was complete and functioning. Our rural area of four counties was one of the last to have been funded by the state legislature, and for the first time Al and I felt that we were not alone in our efforts to find a place to live for our adult-to-be. Barbara now had a counselor and so did we.

There were no homes of quality nearby, and nothing but waiting lists for the Marin County group homes. We thought of the large metropolitan area where Karen and David were now living. David was working as a printer and getting his A.A. degree in graphics, and Karen had started on a two-year R. N. course. That summer Barbara moved close to them and became a city dweller.

She liked the house in which she was to spend the next four years. "Just like Elna's," she commented, referring to her group home in Copenhagen. We, too, had confidence in the overall direction of its philosophy and programs, and the fact that David and Karen were so close to her reassured us. Both of them had grown into observant, responsible advocates for their sister, and she spent much time with them. They dropped by her house and talked to her on the phone. They took her to movies and invited her to dinner. Karen tried to monitor her sister's diet and assumed total responsibility for obtaining her orthopedic boots and leg brace and for keeping them repaired. While Karen was encountering bureaucratic frustrations on her sister's behalf, I was becoming involved in developing a citizen advocacy program, which matches individual volunteer citizens with persons who have developmental special needs and who need support. "Now I know what citizen advocacy is all about," Karen declared one day. "That's what I'm doing for Barbara with her boots and braces." And she was.

Barbara wanted to go to work. All of her life she had gone somewhere away from her home during the daytime hours. She knew that children went to school while adults had jobs like her dad's or attended work activity centers. Like Barbara, I was in enthusiastic agreement with one of the primary objectives of normalization: namely that of the "normal rhythm of life." So Jerry Williams, our regional center counselor, arranged for Barbara to be enrolled in a nearby sheltered workshop. We may have moved too fast in our eagerness. Perhaps we should have let her absorb the shock of a major change of residence before pushing for a vocational program. At any rate, it didn't work out for her. She was bored with a rote work assignment and overwhelmed as well by a somewhat tougher, more assertive group of peers than she was used to. When she began to get into minor fights, the workshop staff and her counselor decided to discontinue her attendance. Sadly she reported to us that she had been "fired." She felt that she had failed.

There was much about her city residence that helped our daughter grow and develop. A new director came in like a breath of fresh air. All the residents adored him, and clothes and spirits brightened. To her dismay Barbara had regained most of the weight that she had so proudly shed the year before. The new young social workers at her group home, however, seemed to understand the devastating effect that her weight was having on her improved self-image and self-confidence, and they promised to help her with diet control and an exercise program. Barbara also learned how to get along with a variety of roommates, some of whom were difficult and disturbed, and this skill should stand her in good stead in the future.

I came to visit her as often as possible on my trips to the city. I happened to be in town on her twenty-first birthday, just a day or two before she was slated to come home for a Christmas vacation. David and I wanted to take her out to lunch and he asked her, "What sort of place would you like, Barbara? Mexican food? Chinese? Hamburgers? You can choose any place you want on your birthday."

She thought hard. "Someplace where we can get a beer!" she announced, fully aware of her new adult status.

We went to a Mexican restaurant and ordered one bottle of beer for the three of us, which we barely managed to finish.

For trips home she had to learn to ride the bus. Often she brought along a friend with whom to share the long journey. There was no direct route, and she had to make a change in San Francisco, where she had to wait for an hour and a half. That was the biggest risk-taking venture for this mother. The bus depot in San Francisco is located in one of the worst sections of town. Only once did she and her girlfriend miss their bus, but they were able to phone and report it to their house. Over and over we talked about the depot, and we rehearsed situations that might occur. I pretended to be a handsome young man who approached her.

"Say, good looking, where are you going?" I'd say.

"Fort Bragg."

"Geez! you don't want to wait all that time. I've got a car. I'm going to Eureka. I'll drive you there." Then I'd ask, "And what are you going to do then, Barbara? Are you going with him?"

I was relieved every time she negotiated the trip safely, and she always did.

When both Karen and David moved away from the city a year later, it made a huge difference in Barbara's level of satisfaction. She felt bereft, in spite of the friends she was making in her residence, and we heard about it whenever she came home. As a matter of fact, we were finding it increasingly difficult to listen to her complain. One time, as we were driving off the freeway towards her house, she looked at me and said, "Ugly, ugly city! What am I doing down here?"

It was David who pulled me up short. We arranged for Barbara to spend occasional weekends with her brother and sister. We decided that she could learn to do this, especially if a friend went with her, and in Barbara's residence there was a young woman whom both David and Karen liked. Their social worker patiently made the reservations, bought tickets, coached the girls, and took them to the airport. Barbara and Jane reported on a fine time, but David's letter gave us cause for concern:

> Barbara and Jane had a nice visit, and I'm sure you
> have heard all the juicy parts. The excitement
> started when I waited at the wrong gate at the air-
> port to meet them. They had me paged, by which
> time I had already realized my mistake. When I

finally met them they were capably on their way to
Travelers' Aid.

We all took the girls out to dinner at friends one
night. They were interested in meeting and talking
with them. Unfortunately Barbara was very quiet
and Jane did all the talking. She does a good job of
mothering her, which is both good and bad.
Barbara seems to accept her role as a child much
too readily. And she acts as if she is very tired
almost all of the time. She sits listlessly, her mind
seeming to drift. Then suddenly her face lights up
for a minute and the old Barbara shines through.
What bothers me even more is the fact that I have
not been taking an active enough part in her life
since moving here, and on these short visits my
patience wears thin 'cause I find it hard to take her
apparent apathy. Maybe you both have some
ideas as to what can be done, or perhaps my
criticism is poorly based. Please comment!

It was an honest letter and one that was not easy for me
to accept. I read it to our regional center counselor and
thought about it a lot. David had hit on a real sore spot.
Once in a moment of anger, a social worker had referred to
me as "only a professional mother." Well, if that was so, I
was certainly compromising my professional principles.
Barbara's residence was, as she had repeatedly said, "Too
big! Too far! And there's nothing to do!" I supposedly
believed in listening to her, and yet I had not done so.

So we began to prepare for another move. Barbara's
counselor and I looked for places that might be suitable
and closer to home. It was not an easy task. One of the
best programs around is located right in our own county
seat, but there is no public transportation to and from the

coast on weekends, and what little there is during the week is still shakily dependent on a county board of supervisors who really don't have their hearts in public transportation. Barbara would have to depend on our driving her back and forth for visits. Looking well into the future, I could see how Al and I might find it difficult to manage an hour-and-half drive each way on foggy, rainy winter nights. Sonoma County, which is south of us by a hundred miles, has a daily bus connection to Fort Bragg. There's no need to worry abut the depots along the way, for they are located in snug little stores or coffee shops, so that is where we began to look in earnest.

Dean Crosthwait, Barbara's new counselor, found two small group homes that seemed well staffed and pro-grammed for increasing their residents' skills in daily living. He arranged for Barbara to spend a long weekend trying the two places. She would stay overnight first in one house and then in the other. She'd visit a couple of work activity centers that might have openings for her. Then Dean would drive her back to the city so that they'd have time to talk about what Barbara had seen. He wanted her to make up her own mind about the three-way choice: to stay at her residence in the city, or to move to Sonoma County and chose between one of the two houses there. She had a month's time to think about it, and Al and I promised Dean to let her talk and to listen to her but to stay out of it as much as possible.

And she did talk about it. One day she came into our bedroom where I was typing and sat quietly near me. I could almost hear the wheels go round in her head.

"What's the matter?" I asked her.

"I'm nervous," she said.

"Worried about moving?"

"Yes, I'll miss my friends," she replied with tears in her voice.

I moved close to her and hugged her. I shared her sadness at parting, but I was delighted that she really was weighing the pros and cons of this heavy decision. I let her tell me about the two houses that she had seen, and then we talked about missing friends, and how we would try to help her keep in touch. I hadn't really thought about this before. It's so easy for most of us to nurture friendships with a letter or a long distance call. We can hop into our cars or arrange for vacation visits. Barbara doesn't have all these options, and it behooves us to keep that in mind.

The house that Barbara chose to move into is one of several group homes referred to as SCILS (Sonoma County Independent Living Skills, Inc.). Until fairly recently, it was a privately owned ranch in Penngrove for boys and young men. As a matter of fact, Barbara was the first woman to move into the residence with four young men—a situation which may well have influenced her decision! It turned out to be a lucky one for more reasons than one. The other house she visited, which was operated by the local parent association for retarded citizens, folded soon afterwards for financial reasons.

The integration process seemed slow, and it worried us a little in the beginning. It seems that one of the highlights of Barbara's trial-run visit had been that the young men had asked her to join them for a Friday evening on the town. They had gone to MacDonald's—Barbara's absolutely favorite dining establishment. Three Fridays passed, and they didn't ask her again. Barbara didn't seem to be concerned, although the house manager and I talked about it. After three Fridays had gone by, we really began to wonder what the problem was, but on the fourth

Friday, it became clear. Barbara's monthly SSI (Supplemental Social Security Income) check caught up with her from the other county, and then they asked her to come along!

Barbara blossomed in her new surroundings. I had hoped that this would happen, but I didn't expect to see the changes happen so fast. Of course, the nearness to Karen had much to do with it. Karen had decided to add a baccalaureate degree in nursing and a family nurse practitioner certification to her two-year R.N. and had moved to Sonoma County. Now she was living two miles down the road from Barbara, and they saw each other often. Just the other day when I phoned Barbara, she sounded breathlessly rushed.

"What's up?" I asked.

"I've gotta go. I'm going bar-hopping with my sister!" (The bar is the local pub on the main street of Penngrove, a village which has become a wide spot in the road since the freeway bypassed it many years ago.)

It's not just Karen, though, or being much closer to home. There are many reasons, both tangible and intangible, for the improved quality of her life. In her new situation the small group principle prevails. Her house is one of several under the SCILS umbrella, but they function independently of one another, and though the residents occasionally party together and visit back and forth, each house is essentially a gathering of individuals. There is no need to sign in or out and though residents and staff persons often take part in social and recreation activities as a group, it's spontaneous planning. If they want to go bowling, they pick up their bags, and inside of five minutes those who want to bowl have left the house. The rest stay at home. There's no need to call out names and check them off a list. There's no filing into a van and then waiting around until heads are counted. It's not a field trip; it's just something one chooses to do for an afternoon or evening.

Compared to the house in the city in which Barbara used to live, the house on Penngrove Avenue is funky. It's a grey stucco in the Italian Swiss style and set back from the road among sheep pastures, old chicken coops, and wooded acres. Each person has a room of his or her own. A local busline stops nearby, and residents can walk to the store, the post office, and the famous pub where many young college students gather. In the daytime everybody leaves for some sort of a work activity. Barbara is learning many different skills at the Casa Grande Center, and though her earnings from recycling cans and bottles are minimal, she saves all the check stubs and proudly shows them off when she comes home.

The staffing and programming are fine. Two house managers live in with the five residents, and there's a third person who covers weekends. A special program consultant is available to assist the staff persons in each of the five houses plan the specific ingredients of each individual's program plan. I've seen her do her work right at the kitchen table, surrounded by supper preparations and unfazed by the confusion. There are no hierarchical distinctions between the social work staff and the house management staff and the residents. Everyone eats together and watches TV together, and if Barbara wants to spend a little time in the house manager's room, she is welcome. I also feel welcome as a parent/advocate/advisor. I can drop in anytime, and it's okay to make suggestions for my daughter's program or welfare.

Many of the staff persons are students, and, as is the

case in most residential situations, they are not earning a generous salary. And yet they work hard. There is a spirit of teamwork and a feeling of accomplishment as each resident is assisted to meet the specific goals in his or her program plan. A written report is prepared four times a year. It goes to the regional center counselor, the work activity center, and to the parents or guardians.

The evaluation report for Barbara charts her progress in cooking skills. It also notes how she is doing with setting the alarm clock, and if anything happens in the morning after it has gone off! There's a report on her thumb-sucking abatement program, her earnest efforts at regulating her diet, how she is getting along with the other residents, and an update on any physical problems that may have required medical attention. As she accomplishes each goal, it is dropped from the program. Soon after Barbara arrived in Penngrove, she relearned how to wash her clothes—a skill that had been lost during the time that she was away from home. We find the reports very helpful. We really know what's going on with our daughter, and we are encouraged to put in our two cents' worth.

Staff training, front-line staff security, career mobility, and adequate reimbursement are at the core of the problems of community living arrangements here in California and all over the country. Private residential facilities— even in the opulent state of California—have a hard time of it. Rates are inadequate for quality programs, and although many residences are supported by the generous efforts of private citizens and well-heeled parents, as well as by public funds, it is difficult for them to make ends meet. So the direct-care staff persons, those who spend the longest and most personal blocks of time with our young adult children in their group homes, are typically kind and humanistically motivated, and yet they are underpaid, undertrained persons who have to learn on the job. Orientation frequently consists of following another staff person around for a day or two.

Soon after Barbara settled in at Penngrove, Karen wrapped up the situation in one sentence: "The difference is that they really like Barbara here!" She didn't intend this as a criticism of the staff in Barbara's previous living situation, but rather as an affirmation of what can be done when staff persons know what they are doing and can measure the outcome of their best efforts. They can accomplish small miracles, and their relationships with residents become deep and joyful because they are not burned out by impossible expectations or bored by having no expectations at all.

The changes in our girl began to show up on her very first weekend visit home. She was clearly more animated, sat up taller, and had more to say to us about all sorts of happenings. She hadn't volunteered to help for ages, and I had grown accustomed to dragging her out of the big black armchair. Now she stood in the kitchen, saying "Can I do the dishes?" proudly, for she knows once more that she can wash dishes competently. When she dug out the shoe shine kit and announced that she was about to clean her boots, I couldn't believe my eyes. Those boots hadn't been cleaned in a long, long time.

During the very first month of her new venture, Barbara got dumped by a bus on her way to work. The driver pulled out too fast as she was getting on too slowly. She was battered and bruised and quite scared, but she was urged to continue riding the bus, and she is learning more routes all the time, as part of the community exploration program at the work center. When she and one of her housemates missed the last bus after the movie and dawdled around for quite a while before phoning the house for a ride, she was grounded for a week, and to my knowledge has learned her lesson.

Since her move, Barbara has been well and happy most of the time. When she had the doldrums last fall, her house manager suggested that a new hairdo might cheer her up, and she surprised us all at Christmas with a brand-new wash 'n wear permanent.

I asked Barbara herself if she would tell me what's good about living at Penngrove. She said, "I like the boys—and we ride the bus." She still speaks of her city friends and misses them, and we have arranged for her friend Jane to come and spend the night with her. When Karen and her friends drive to the city, Barbara sometimes goes along to visit her former residence.

We wonder, of course, about Barbara's future. We worry about how long she will be able to stay in the house at Penngrove and about the permanence of SCILS as a private nonprofit organization in the land of Proposition 13. I have concerns about the goal of independent living as the ideal end-all of her training. Barbara has told me that she will be going into an apartment. Perhaps she could, but would she really want to? I have just realized that never in my sixty-two years have I lived all by myself. I've been alone, yes, but I've always shared my living quarters with parents, friends, fellow students, or my husband and children. And why do some perfectly able adults choose to live in residence clubs?

Total independence may mean loneliness. I prefer Bob Perske's concept of "interdependence," which means growth, development, and support. Eight years ago in

Denmark, Elna Skov was already thinking about this. One of her residents who graduated to a place of her own had crumbled under the pressure. They found her refrigerator smelly, her place a mess, and even her personal grooming had gone downhill. She moved back into the group home, and the staff did not think that she would be capable of living out again. As a matter of fact, she rallied, but the point is that the program was flexible enough to provide a period of relief and rehabilitation.

I find that it is normal for our energies to ebb and flow. Life stages and crises cause all of us to be more or less capable of independence. Living arrangements for our sons and daughters must take this into account, so that they can know the excitement of risk and growth as well as the peace of mind that comes from having as little or as much support as they may need.

13 *A Map For The Future*

IN THE PAST EVERYONE assumed that those with special needs had to live in separate, special places. We still put old people in large nursing or convalescent homes and re-tarded people in institutions, villages, or residences, where we bring special services to them. Classes, work-shops, mini-buses, beauty parlors, soda fountains—all are expensive facilities and programs duplicating those that already exist in the mainstream. Still today we arbi-trarily designate human beings as being too profoundly retarded to live with the rest of us. For them we beef up the institutions and then lull ourselves with the smug sat-isfaction of having enriched their lives. Those residents of institutions whom we classify as having community po-tential we train and groom in preparation for reentry into the outside world. We expect them to earn their way out, when the emphasis should be on tooling up and readying the hometown for their rightful return.

How many of us, healthy today, may have to live out our lives in a little room opening onto the long, smelly corridor of a nursing home when an accident, a stroke, or a degenerative disease renders us speechless, nonambu-lant, or incontinent? Would we not prefer a life of dignity close to our families, supported by "meals on wheels," a homemaker, or a visiting nurse? It is no different for persons with developmental disabilities, and their potential for growth is tremendous.

By expanding existing social services with programs that work, we can welcome back all of those who live in large institutions. We can forever prevent further placements in them. We can give families needed support and offer children and young adults living situations that will keep them with or near their families and friends.

Since the early 1950s we have developed an impressive body of knowledge and practical experience, much of which is based on the principle of the "developmental model." In everyday language this means that one success leads to another. It's so simple that we tend to forget it. Everybody learns by learning! For people with developmental special needs, it becomes their lifeline. Each solidly learned skill is an accomplishment that boosts their self-confidence and self-esteem and leads to mastery of the next skill in the sequence. For the parents of children with these needs, it strengthens their proud resolve to keep their children at home.

There are excellent programs based on the developmental model here and there, but they are still much too widely scattered and woefully underfunded. If only we could put these fine programs together, if we could cover the map of the United States with them, then I would worry less about the future.

Many people—parents, professionals, legislators, and bureaucrats—are going to have to change their beliefs and attitudes so it will happen.

Recently, First Lady Rosalynn Carter requested information on programs that really work with mentally retarded children and adults. The President's Committee on Mental Retardation enlisted the talents of Robert and Martha Perske to highlight and illustrate some of these programs. Bob went scurrying through the entire country to see for himself. The report to the president, *Mental Retardation: The Leading Edge—Service Programs that Work,* is now complete and should charge us with great hope and optimism. My map of the future is still far from covered with exemplary programs but, as Bob says, "It's like the parts of the car are all over the garage floor. All we have to do now is put them together!"

According to projections made by the President's Committee on Mental Retardation, the incidence of mental retardation could be cut in half by the end of this century if we practiced all we know. If we could wipe out all pockets of poverty, eliminate cultural deprivation, and provide love, security, and care for all children, we would prevent many disabling conditions.

It seems like an overwhelming task, but we can tackle parts of it relatively easily. We know more about the ideal age for child bearing, for instance, than we did twenty years ago. Young girls under seventeen and women over thirty-five are more likely than others to have babies with developmental special needs. We must take this information into the classrooms of our nation's schools and couple it with other health information. It is important for young men and women to take care of their bodies now and to take responsibility for the health of their children-to-be before they become sexually active. Many teen-agers who become pregnant are afraid to admit it, and several crucial months go by before their unborn babies are given the prenatal care they should have. Since three months of pop and potato chips can do irreversible harm, the value of nutrition must be taught. In my generation pregnant women were warned against gaining more than twelve to twenty pounds. The pendulum of knowledge is swinging back towards the "eating for two" theory of earlier days as being much better for the baby.

For people who have a sibling with a developmental disability, it is possible to obtain genetic counseling and preconception tests. If a person at risk is already pregnant, there is a procedure called amniocentesis which can diagnose certain abnormalities of the fetus inside the uterus.

I'm sure I would have availed myself of amniocentesis if it had been available twenty-five years ago and if I had known that I was a mother at risk because of my age. Would I have chosen an abortion if I had been told of the possibility of an abnormality? It's hard to second-guess a decision I did not have to make at the time, and it is precisely at this point that prevention becomes a difficult ethical question. Barbara is alive and a real person, and were I to answer yes, it would seem like a retroactive death wish for a member of our family whom we love and value. Yet I firmly believe that biochemists and physicians will continue to ask why children are born with impairments, deformities, and pathologies. They will continue to want to "prevent" these problems in the dictionary sense of the word: to forestall, hinder, keep from happening. I want the researchers to continue, for much as Barbara has deepened my awareness of the human condition and broadened my horizon, I also realize that she has been cheated of much pleasure, and I would have wished a more trouble-free life for her.

At a state convention of parent associations in 1971, we were told by genetics experts from the University of California at San Diego that they had come up with new identifiable chromosomal causes of mental retardation. They were encouraging us, as high risk families, to make use of this knowledge. Al and I decided to have a chromosome study done which might throw some light on the cause of Barbara's condition, which until then had been unknown.

If there was one thing Barbara hated, it was needles, and Al and I were put in the position of trying to explain why she had to let the doctor take some blood out of her arm and send it to the lab. We didn't want to say that there was something wrong with her and that we wouldn't want Karen and David to have a child like her. That was more than she should have to deal with. Since we knew that she was aware of her problems with learning, speech, and co-ordination, we said that the blood test might tell doctors why she had those problems and then they might be able to help new babies grow up without them. Barbara accepted this explanation, but the tests showed no chromosomal abnormality.

There are other kinds of mental retardation that can be prevented by prompt action after the baby's birth and during the early years of childhood. A simple blood test right after birth shows whether or not there is evidence of phenylketonuria (PKU), which causes serious, irreversible mental retardation if undetected and untreated. California and forty-four other states mandate this test, but they do not yet have a law which would require that it be extended to check for six other diseases which also cause mental retardation that are preventable when treated early. Besides PKU, galactosemia, maple syrup urine disease, histidinemia, homocystinuria, tyrosinemia, and hypothyroidism can be prevented if a single drop of blood, taken from the heel of the newborn, is sent to a well-equipped lab. We must bring political pressure to bear to demand these preventive measures.

And there are other preventive issues in which we can become involved and about which we must spread the word. Lead poisoning is still a problem in our country. Although the federal Lead-Based Paint, Lead Poisoning Control Act has done a tremendous job of stopping the manufacture of paints containing lead, there still exist deteriorating buildings where kids can pick off the new safe paint and reach layers of lead paint underneath. We must continue to monitor paint production and see to it that old slum buildings are replaced with decent housing.

Lead poisoning, we now know, does not come from eating lead-based paint alone. Much of it is caused by the exhaust from cars and other vehicles. Dr. Robert Guthrie, Professor of Pediatrics and Microbiology, State University of New York at Buffalo, is quoted in *The Leading Edge* as follows:

> The Federal Environmental Agency reports that one of the major sources of lead poisoning in the past two decades—affecting small children—comes from the tremendous contamination of soil and dust by the exhaust of tetraethyl lead from our automobiles. . . .
>
> One health department professional in California, testing the soil downwind from one of the freeways, found that one percent of the dry weight of the top soil was lead. Well, if you have ever watched children play in dirt, and when you know that a child ingesting only a micro-amount of this soil will receive a severe case of lead poisoning, you can't help but become alarmed.

205

There is also a need for continuing public education about vaccination programs for German measles, red measles, and polio. The public needs to know that Rh factor problems can be solved. New parents should be informed of the importance of using safe car seats for their infants and toddlers. Infants and small children are especially vulnerable to brain damage as a result of car accidents, since the disproportionate weight of their heads tends to increase the force of impact when there is a collision or a sudden stop. The parent association in Ukiah, California, has launched a car seat information program, coupled with a car seat exchange. There is a great difference in quality, cost, and safety factors of which parents should be aware, and an exchange program can be an effective means of increasing their use.

In spite of all these Trojan preventive efforts, we may never totally win the battle. The human condition will, no doubt, continue to bring us some children with developmental special needs. There will be children who have accidents or get into things that harm or poison them. We have learned that early diagnosis and intervention are our best preventive efforts and if we continue to improve the quality of programs for these children and the attitude of society towards them, their lives will be worth living—as they should be.

Developmental disabilities, of course, do not always appear at birth or during early infancy. They can be caused by poisoning, by a very high fever or by accident. Unfortunately, the federal definition of "developmental disability" states that the condition must have existed before a person reaches the age of twenty-two. If persons older than that become disabled, they do not have access to those programs and services which are funded for persons with mental retardation, cerebral palsy, epilepsy, autism, and other conditions defined by law. It doesn't seem fair or right, and I hope that the time will come when health services will be given according to specific needs instead of specific diagnoses.

But let's imagine, for a moment, an ideal situation for parents of a child born with a disability. Help is available right after the baby's birth when medical and nursing personnel have been well trained in counseling parents. Instead of postponing the discussion or glossing over the problem, the physician gently but honestly breaks the news to both mother and father. There is no talk of getting a second opinion or of putting the baby away in a state institution. At this moment, the new parents may be totally incapable of understanding scientific explanations, but they can feel warmth and caring. They have hope and can place trust in the promise of future support. Later, when their pain and shock have lessened, they are given opportunities to talk and ask questions. Their nurses and doctors know the resources available in the community, and the team approach begins.

Parents who have been there themselves may be the best line of defense. In Omaha, Nebraska, new parents of a developmentally disabled child can be put in contact with experienced parents within twenty-four hours, thanks to an organization called Pilot Parents. Members of the group offer emotional support as peers rather than as counselors, and they help parents find services for their children. When a service is not available, they become advocates for providing it. At the time *The Leading Edge* reported on the program, there were forty-five Pilot Parents, sixteen of whom had graduated from being receivers of assistance to being givers of it.

One of California's chief resources for parents is a network of twenty-one regional centers. As defined by state law, they provide central locations where individuals with developmental disabilities or their families can obtain needed services or be referred to them. The regional centers provide diagnosis and coordination of such resources as education, health, welfare, rehabilitation, and recreation. Other states are providing the needed services too. Washington State's Bureau of Developmental Disabilities offers access to a variety of in-home services such as respite care, therapy, program skill development, and government-subsidized parent-to-parent contacts.

As part of their early counseling, parents should be taken on a conducted tour of nearby developmental programs so that they can replace a stereotyped view of persons with handicaps with more hopeful impressions of children in schools and adults at work, who are making the kind of progress that they may expect for their own child. They must be assured of community support and a direction for their baby from the very beginning.

Infants with severe multiple handicaps require life support services that may not be available in their home-town. But, even for the baby who requires complex medical intervention, the ultimate aim should be to make a return home possible.

In Omaha, Nebraska, such a life support program is located on one floor of a large, modern county hospital. It is bright, cheerful, and moving in both senses of the word! Severely disabled infants and small children are surrounded by colorful wall decorations, huge floor pillows, music, and a wide variety of prosthetic devices. They are constantly stimulated, touched, and loved on a one-to-one basis, and they improve. Recently, one little girl with arrested hydrocephaly and other major problems was enrolled in an integrated preschool class of unimpaired and handicapped children in the public schools of Omaha.

The team approach which is brought to bear on these children involves physicians, nurses, teachers, speech and physical therapists, counselors, social workers, and, of course, parents. Parents help with feeding and bathing, and they take their child home for weekend trial runs before he or she is ready and able to return home for good. The progress of the children in this program has been so convincing that staff persons now want to establish similar services in smaller, more localized units.

Five years ago, when Tom and Sunny Whalley, the parents of a profoundly handicapped son and two teenage daughters, moved to a larger house in Carmichael, California, they founded the Somerset Home School, a twenty-four-hour training unit for six profoundly handicapped youngsters. Tom and Sunny hold the respective positions of administrator and program director, and there are four child care workers. The school has access to the services of a physical therapist, nutritionist, case workers from the regional center, and a registered nurse.

Like the hospital in Omaha, Somerset is far more than a place where services are delivered. According to *The Leading Edge,*

> Frail, multi-handicapped children come into a three-acre wonderland of sensory stimulation and the reinforcement of healthy responses to it. The house is filled with bright colors, harmonious music, restful waterbeds, voices with loving tones, hands that massage, arms that hold one close, the stimulating waters of a Jacuzzi whirlpool, the

smell of bread and a noisy canary. Outside is the sun, fresh air, a swimming pool, two spirited horses, a gentle pony, goats, dogs, cats, a rabbit and a duck. All play an important part in giving direction to these children's lives.

The training program itself is intense:

Detailed interventions of Neurodevelopmental Training (NDT) are carried out faithfully. For example, body positioning and head control programs continue all day. The jerky infantile reflexes—so important at birth but an impediment to growth if they fail to diminish—are helped to fade, while the purposeful use of lips, tongue and jaw are stimulated and reinforced. . . . All efforts are geared to helping the children move from weakness to strength, from negative behaviors to purposeful interactions with the world around them. Their progress is measured by precision charting of behaviors, as well as by monthly videotapes.

The aim of Somerset Home School is to provide every appropriate early childhood intervention and to involve the family increasingly so that a stronger, more valued child will return to his or her own home. In his glowing report on the program, Robert Perske casts a vote for parental action:

There is hope for the mentally retarded when the parents of such children—people like the

Whalleys—refuse to accept what others believe about their handicapped child. In this case, a family has ignored the pessimistic presumption that profoundly handicapped children must be written off as having no future at all. . . . Salvaging destinies is a supremely difficult business but it can be done.

Only 5 percent of the babies born with developmental disabilities fall into the profoundly handicapped range. Newborns with less severe disabilities are usually able to go home from the hospital after a few days. From this point on, an array of family support services should be provided as needed. If the baby has special medical problems such as cerebral palsy, the public health nurse will be of tremendous assistance. Home aides can help with bathing, toilet training, feeding, and dressing skills, and parents should be shown how to teach them to their child.

Infant stimulation is an important part of the in-home support program. A baby who has had a traumatic birth, a serious illness, or seems delayed in developing may need a lot of encouragement. Barbara inadvertently showed us the way to a haphazard stimulation program by responding to excitement and the lack of routine. Now there are experts who can come into the home and teach families how to enrich their baby's environment so that he or she may catch up, or at least not fall too far behind, other children of the same age. Infant stimulation includes motor, language, and play activities, which help a child "learn to move" so that he or she can "move to learn." Stimulation can range from a mobile over a crib to tickling a child or rolling him on a waterbed, and it's not a mother-only program. It's a family affair in which Dad and siblings take an active part.

Every baby deserves the chance to do his or her best, and the most important time for learning to see, hear, touch, move, and talk is between birth and six years of age. There are many variations on the theme of infant stimulation—some in the home and others in small cooperative parent groups where babies with problems, siblings, parents, and counselors all learn together. The ones I've seen were confusingly animated, and I couldn't tell the problem squirmers from their brothers and sisters! Here in Fort Bragg we now have a "toybrary" where parents can meet while their children play to learn about child development, discuss mutual problems, and find out about various toys and their specific uses. Then they may check out the toys and take them home on a loan basis.

All of this activity is pretty strenuous stuff, which puts a great overload on the family both physically and emotionally. All the attention is focused on the baby, and nobody smiles anymore. There are few picnics, and no weekend trips at all. No one seems to have time to talk about kindergarten or Little League. And for the married couple it's good-bye to square dancing, bridge, and dinner out with friends. Even a normally relaxed sex life may seem unattainable. That's what respite is all about. As far as I'm concerned it's the essential family support service. Respite care enables the family to resume as normal a life as possible as soon after the baby's birth as possible. The family needs a break early before strain and tensions undermine relationships.

Respite can be an in-home service provided by a baby-sitter trained in caring for a child with a disability or a place to which the handicapped child can go for a longer period of time. Parents may take off for a weekend by themselves or plan an afternoon with their other children. Even a bath taken at one's ease without having to keep one ear cocked for catastrophic events can be total luxury!

Strangely enough, we are still encountering difficulties in launching respite programs. There is an expressed need for this service, but a reluctance on the part of families to ask for it once it comes into existence. We have searched for reasons. I have a hunch that it may be the result of our splendid but erroneous do-it-yourself philosophy. Do it yourself! Conquer the pain! Suffer 'till you're numb! It's a far cry from the neighborly help exchanged by our pioneer ancestors.

Because of the isolation and confusion of life in our large towns and cities, respite services do require some structure, organization, and funding, but this expense should be seen as our society's legitimate investment in the future stability of families. Families who have children with special problems should be offered this support freely and should not be made to feel guilty about asking for it. In time a family in need of respite may become a pillar of strength to someone else.

I would go one step further and recommend a family subsidy program which reimburses parents for the extra cost of raising a disabled child or children in their own home and which recompenses them for the skills they acquire. It has been found that both natural and foster parents proudly take training which teaches them to coordinate the often complex programs and schedules of a child with special needs. It's happening at the Macomb/ Oakland Regional Center in Michigan, where people are strengthening their parenting skills in special training courses and then putting these skills to work in their own homes. In Orange County, California, parents have the opportunity to enter a training program which qualifies them as program coordinators for their own children.

All this seems like a strong and healthy step in the right direction, especially when I remember the days when parents were accused of being anxious when we showed concern for our children. At the time the chasm between professional expertise and parental built-in know-how seemed to be unbridgeable.

The most visible change in public services for the handicapped since Barbara was a little girl is in the area of education. Even in my glummest moments, I can take comfort in that. Today's family with a handicapped child can stand squarely on U.S. Public Law 94-142, the Education for All Handicapped Children Act. They can battle any bureaucrats who say that they are not able to comply, for the law went into effect nationwide in the school year 1979/80.

When Barbara was small, the public school people argued that retarded children should start school later than other children because their mental age was lower than their chronological age. Age eight was recommended. In contrast to this, PL 94-142 states that the handicapped child's education must begin early if it is to be effective: age three is the mandate. In a few bright spots on our map of the United States, there are educators who want to bring handicapped children into the school system even earlier than that.

In Madison, Wisconsin, any child from birth to five years who is handicapped or at risk may become a public school student. One parent enrolled his daughter twenty-five minutes after she was born! At first, a special education teacher comes to the home at regular intervals to help the parents develop a training program. As soon as the child is ready, he or she attends one of three elementary schools for early childhood instruction. In *The Leading Edge* Robert Perske states emphatically, "There is no attempt, in any of the three schools, to conduct the programs 'off to the side.' Instead, the students, teachers and parents are accepted as an integral part of the schools' program." This is the way he describes one of the schools:

> At Spring Harbor the classrooms—located in the middle of the building have brightly colored walls and rugs and an abundance of toys and play equipment. In this attractive setting, professionals, parents and elementary school students help 35 children overcome or compensate for such problems as hydrocephaly, Down's Syndrome, cerebral palsy, spina bifida, and the absence of speech, sight, hearing, arms or legs. Thirty percent of the children are severely and profoundly handicapped.

I realize that the very word "mainstreaming" often puts teachers and administrators into a flap. It is still a hotly debated, controversial concept. We may say that it is now the law of the land, but when teachers protest that we are dumping children into already overcrowded classrooms, they have a point. And when they are fearful and out of their depth, we have failed to explain the resources that should be available to them as children with disabilities are placed in their classes. We have rushed in when patient preparation would have served us better. In Madison, the school district spent an entire year preparing teachers, students, and parents before attempting programs such as the one described above.

For the sake of families of the future, I hope that PL 94-142 will succeed so that disabled children will go to school alongside their lucky peers who happen to have been born healthy and whole. I believe that our country has the resources and the ingenuity to work out the technical and administrative details.

Until recently, the principle of segregation has operated in the workplace as well as in the schools. We have limited most handicapped people to long-term sheltered work instead of preparing them for mainstream employment according to their abilities. Good job performance provides a tremendous boost to the self-esteem of disabled workers, and it may well be the key to the public's changed view of them. A used-car dealer taught me that lesson.

After several meetings with a vocational rehabilitation counselor, he had agreed to employ a young man from the sheltered workshop as a car washer. Several weeks went by, and the counselor dropped by the lot to inquire about his client. "How is Jim Walsh doing, Mr. Jones?" he asked.

"Jim Walsh? I don't seem to recall—"

The counselor's heart sank. "You know—the young man I placed here from the workshop to try out for the car wash job."

"Oh yeah? Jim! I remember now. He's doing okay. He's one of us now."

New training techniques are making it possible to provide meaningful work for persons with disabilities. We can now break down complex tasks into small components so that they can be done by persons who were once considered incapable of remunerative work. The film, *Try Another Way*, which explains Marc Gold's training method in task analysis, poignantly illustrates the difference meaningful work can make in the lives of severely disabled persons.

Two California programs for persons who now produce with pride, although they may never be able to compete on their own, are described in *The Leading Edge*. The first, a community redevelopment program in Los Angeles, has been so successful in its services to the community that it has continued since a federal grant ran out in 1977. It consists of work crews made up of five mentally retarded adults and a nonhandicapped lead worker. The lead workers are paid with funds provided through the Comprehensive Employment Training Act (CETA) and the other workers receive a small monthly stipend from the local regional center in addition to their Supplemental Security Incomes (SSI). According to one lead worker, "Some of the fellows take home blueprints and spread them out on the kitchen table to show their dads what they're doing. They may not be able to read the words, but they can point to the various components and describe them. For some of the workers, this has been the first time their fathers ever took an interest in anything they did." According to the project director, "We've learned never to underestimate the personal values that come from wearing a tool belt, a hard hat and having one's own tool box. These items tell others that a guy stands ready to perform no-nonsense labor that can even be dangerous."

The second is a private business founded by the parent of a retarded young adult. Al Filipponi invested all he had in the Donut Shop of La Mesa, California.

> The business employs three bakers, five sales-persons, an administrator and a vocational teacher. An average of 12 mentally retarded vocational trainees work side by side with the regular employees in this unique, learn-by-doing enterprise. A small house behind the Donut Shop has been converted into a classroom where the trainees participate in job-related learning activities.

The shop is a thriving commercial success, which is also providing invaluable experience to all those who are working to make it prosper.

In spite of the progress that is being made, there are still plenty of tasks left with which families of handicapped children can test their patience and perseverance. All of our exemplary, courageous new programs give us goals to shoot for, but even so, life won't move along smoothly all the time, not for Barbara or for the young families of tomorrow. It is for this reason that parents ask their ever-present question, "What will happen to our child when we're gone?" and it is for this reason that citizen advocacy came into being.

The term refers to a responsible relationship in which a concerned citizen is the advocate for a person who has a developmental disability such as mental retardation, epilepsy, cerebral palsy, or autism. Always volunteers, advocates support the emotional and practical needs of their friend and assist in his or her growth to greater independence. I first read about it in 1971, shortly after our return from Denmark, and it seemed like the ideal program for the many persons with developmental problems who were forever falling through the cracks of our fragmented service systems. The idea underlying the concept is as basic as the salt of the earth and as necessary as our daily bread: people solving human problems by lending a hand when and where they're needed.

Citizen advocacy has grown from the original scholarly schema into workable programs that offer individualized support, which public service agencies cannot possibly deliver to the hundreds of people on their case load.

The concept of citizen advocacy is the brainchild of Wolf Wolfensberger, an internationally renowned professional in the mental retardation field. When I first met Wolf, I was a little awed by this intense, articulate man. But then I spent an evening with him and a dozen young people who were doing volunteer work with the Association for Retarded Citizens and watched them react to his infectious missionary zeal and enthusiasm. Many hours later, these young people were ready to venture forth and launch citizen advocacy programs for their friends with problems.

Wolf teaches leadership and advocacy courses for human services personnel throughout the United States and Canada. His recent speeches at conventions tend to be fiery doomsday messages about abuses in institutions, hospitals, and nursing homes, not only for our constituents, but also for thousands of elderly Americans. He draws distressing parallels to concentration and prison camps. It's depressing stuff, and many parents and professionals don't want to hear it, but my friend Barbara Jessing in Omaha recently took a three-day course from Wolfensberger and wrote, "I had forgotten what a good teacher Wolf is. For the first time in months I went out Monday morning all charged up with my work and knowing why I was doing it!"

The concept of advocacy on behalf of people with developmental disabilities has been written into law. United States Public Law 94-103, Section 113, mandates that "every state will have in effect a system to protect and advocate the rights of persons with developmental disabilities by 1977, and that such system will have the authority to pursue legal, administrative and other appropriate remedies to insure the protection of the rights of such persons who are receiving treatment, services or habilitation by the state, and be independent of any State agency which provides treatment, services or habilitation to persons with developmental disabilities."

Though the money appropriated by the federal government is a relatively small amount, protection and advocacy agencies are beginning to make their presence known. California's toll-free hotline in the Sacramento office of Protection and Advocacy, Inc., rings often, and I have high hopes that such agencies will fulfill the intent of the law, so that every citizen with a developmental disability will be able to reach outside the service-providing systems of their state in order to obtain their rights and entitlements.

Many years ago I read that one out of ten persons in this country is affected by the existence of someone who has developmental special needs, and I am convinced that the base of involved people has since broadened. There are siblings, camp counselors, respite workers, teacher's aides, students, social workers, and therapists—innumerable young people who are entering the field of human services, and on whom I base my hope for Barbara's future. They have grown up to believe in a concept which is most eloquently expressed in California's Senate Resolution No. 30 of 1972, introduced by Senator Clair Burgener:

RESOLVED BY THE SENATE OF THE STATE OF CALIFORNIA THE ASSEMBLY THEREOF CONCURRING,

That the Legislature hereby declares that the mentally retarded person has a right to as normal a life as possible despite the severity of his handicap and should be afforded the same basic rights as other citizens of California of the same age;

and be it further RESOLVED, That "normalization" is defined to mean that despite any limitations, each retarded individual shall be provided the maximum opportunity to participate in usual living experiences including education, work, and social activities that permit development to his highest potential,

and be it further RESOLVED, That such opportunity for "normalization" is the birthright of every citizen and a proper investment for the good of society.

It is going to take many more years of hard work to make it happen. Many of us will have to join forces. We need a strong coalition of informed and concerned parents, and friends and neighbors as well, who really believe in the basic fact that people grow and develop and that they rise to high expectations.

At present, a new force is surfacing and joining the coalition. People First and other self-advocacy groups are made up of persons who have developmental disabilities, but who are tired of living lives planned for and directed by others. People First originated in Oregon and is now springing up in other states under a variety of names.

This spring I attended California's first People First convention in San Francisco. I met Barbara by accident in a large meeting room filled with a couple of hundred of the liveliest, most enthusiastic delegates I have ever seen. She wanted to make a speech but turned around at the last minute and walked back across the platform to where I was standing. "I chickened out!" she said, and I told her that there would be another time for speaking out. Speaking up for oneself, or self-advocating as we call it, is another learned skill, just like making choices. Years ago, I was overwhelmed by the ease with which my fellow students in New York could express their thoughts and even argue with professors. I was nervous, too!

I have no doubt that Barbara will be making speeches. People First is setting the pace for self-advocates in learning to organize meetings, take part in discussions, appearing on TV, and talking with legislators. I hope that its members will be invited to join coalitions wherever they organize chapters. I hope that they will have opportunities to fill out consumer surveys, in which they will have a chance to give their own assessment of services provided to them. With People First as allies, parents and citizen advocates stand a better chance of convincing local, state, and federal officials that we need more funds for family support programs in our communities. The very existence of this organization shows that these programs pay off, because they help individuals become more independent as well as giving families a chance to hang together. Local rather than institutional programs are cost beneficial and good for the communities they serve. We have moved well beyond the question, "Do community programs work?" The question now is, "How can we help make them work?"

14 *Dear Barbara*

I WISH I COULD PROMISE you the good life. I wish it for you, for Jeff, Susan, Terry, Eddie, Raymond, Evelyn, Lucy, Micky, and thousands of others. The good life would be in or near your hometown with all the ups and downs that should be a part of "allbody's" life.

Parents want health, wealth, success, and everything nice for their children. And yet we can only wish, never promise. You and I have often talked about this, mostly when you have become impatient because nothing in your life seems to be going right. I know how much you yearn, like other people, for real work and a special boy friend. You wish you had a driver's license and the freedom to move here and there as your brother and sister do.

It makes me furious to see you sit slumped over with your thumb in your mouth when I know that you can sit tall and look animated. I glow when you are at your shiniest best, seeing something that needs to be done and doing it without being told. I can see the direct relationship between our programs for you and your growth. When we fail to provide you with these supports and opportunities, our failure becomes your own, and that is the ultimate cop-out.

Then I tell you that the good life takes effort. That all your many allies cannot work miracles without your help.

"It's not going to happen if you do a sloppy job," I'll say to you. "The good life is a team effort which happens only when everybody pulls together."

Nobody has ever accused you of being an overly enthusiastic worker, Barbara, but you spell recreation with a capital *R*. For many years now, we've watched you have a good time at both parties with your peers and mixed events. You have that warm, spontaneous capacity for putting people at their ease when they are made momentarily uncomfortable by your different speech and appearance. Just recently, Karen tells me, you spoke to a leather-jacketed, tough-looking type at a dance. He softened and chatted with you for fifteen minutes.

We probably would not have taken you to Europe with us last year if you had not spoken up. You had been there with us before, and now you wanted to come along. "I wanna go, too," you said. "I wanna see my friends in Denmark and visit my cousins."

We had to consider two factors. First there was the additional cost. We put aside that thought after I remembered a discussion I had had long ago with Karen at a time when your annual summer camp fee had taken a sudden jump. "Don't ever let me hear you complain about money for Barbara," she had said. "Don't you realize how much more you spend for David and for me for fun things and school affairs? Barbara hardly ever gets to go anywhere!"

Then we wondered if you could do it. Would you enjoy the many strange places? Would your flat feet and leg brace hold you back?

Once more, we took a chance, and it worked out. In fact, it turned out to be a tremendous learning experience for you and for us. Your friendly, one-line introduction, "My name's Barbara—what's yours?" leaped across the language barriers of six European countries. By the end of six weeks you were becoming expert at climbing steep steps, carrying your suitcase long distances, and balancing along wobbly train corridors. We stretched your endurance, energy, and attention time and time again, and you responded by becoming more alert and observant and sharper and brighter.

It was the kind of glow point which happens only once in a while but which lights up a life for a long time. We enjoyed one another's company and shared experiences as friends. It was an exciting adult adventure, which the perennial summer camp had ceased to provide. So for you and your friends in the future, I wish vacations of all sorts: trips to other countries, camping, visits to resorts, and lots of sight-seeing.

You're in a good vocational training program now. One day you cook, another you garden. You smash cans at the recycling center and learn to find your way around town. Yet I hear you say that you want a real job, and perhaps that, too, will be possible for you in the future. As your mother, I'm too constrained by my dreams and my love for you to be a fair judge of your employability. I do believe, however, that there are a great many things left for you to learn, even though you're not ambitious, and your weight and feet tend to slow you down.

I'm sure that our sheltered workshops and work activity centers need to be better funded so that they can employ more staff persons who receive continuing training in new methods. We need to employ supervisors who can establish work stations in industry so that you and your peers can be trained in real factories, hospitals, motels, and nursery schools, depending on your interests and preparation. We need to begin vocational training early in school and strengthen the process in adulthood. I hope yours didn't start too late in your life. I fear that a period of national economic depression will hurt our work programs, and I know that "real work" gives you pride, as it does most people in our society.

When you were a child, I was astounded that our work ethic rubbed off on you so readily. It took me awhile to understand that mental retardation did not reduce your capacity to receive messages from our society. Now I believe that you and your peers are more sensitive than the rest of us. I remember how excited you were when we applied for your Supplemental Security Income (SSI) allotment. When we gave you a power mower for exercise and fresh air, you negotiated for wages every time you cut the grass in the backyard. Now, when you are home for weekends, you want your Dad to bring home collating work for you to do and you expect to be paid.

How could we have been so unobservant? After all, we live in a culture in which occupational success is considered all important. "What do you do?" follows hot on the heels of the first introduction, and sheltered work somehow doesn't count for as much as being "a tinker, a tailor, a candlestick maker."

Now that you're living away from home, we see a change in you. You are no longer our docile little girl. From time to time you speak up politely but firmly. A few months ago when you had just come home for the weekend and we had company for dinner, I asked you to take the soup bowls off the table. "I'm not your maid," was your smiling reply, as you got up and did it. When I was your guest for supper at Penngrove, I said a few grumbling words about the butter on your potato and the mayonnaise on the artichoke. You looked me squarely in the eye and put me right in my place. "This is my house!" you said. As we drove home to Fort Bragg later that evening, I was negotiating a freeway on-ramp when I heard you say something. I didn't reply because I was concentrating on the traffic. "Hey!" you said as you nudged me, "I asked you something!" We see such assertiveness as healthy signs of your strengthening personhood.

I think you're lucky, Barbara, for you will have Karen and David as your guardians when your father and I are dead. Both of them understand your program needs and know what you're entitled to. When your counselors, teachers, and house manager sit down together to plan your individual program, Karen or David will be informed members of that team. Your dad and I have no qualms at all about their capability as guardians. We feel confident that they will not abuse the arrangement nor infringe on your rights unnecessarily.

Guardianship—based as it is in California on a declaration of incompetence—technically deprives the ward of many opportunities such as money contracts, changing residence without permission, and marriage. It is being questioned these days as a violation of rights because in many cases wards are not given their legal right to appear in court and approve or contest the appointment of their own guardian. As a consequence, their property rights are sometimes abridged. In spite of this, Al and I have designated Karen and David to be your guardians in our wills, for we trust them to carry out their guardianship of you in our spirit.

We not only trust them, but we also rely on them to be anchors in your future life. That may not be fair to them unless they, too, have help. They have lives of their own to live, and we wish you would not have to depend totally on them for emotional support. While you will probably continue to live in familiar northern California, they may be called elsewhere by wanderlust, the demands of their careers, or affairs of the heart. So be it. All three of you deserve your own time and space so that you will continue to come together willingly and in respect and love.

A good home, meaningful work, a healthy independence, and love of family is what we wish for you, Barbara, just as we hope Karen and David will have those things, too. We wish you well—all of you—with the words of e. e. cummings:

> here is the deepest secret nobody knows
> (here is the root of the root and the bud of the bud
> and the sky of the sky of a tree called life;which grows
> higher than soul can hope or mind can hide)
> and this is the wonder that's keeping the stars apart
>
> i carry your heart(i carry it in my heart)*

And I intend to carry it with me straight into the hereafter. I wish I knew exactly what life is going to be like for you after Al and I are gone. Like so many conditions in your life, over which you have only curtailed control, the hereafter is impossible for me to explain to you. "I don't know" isn't good enough for something as irrevocable and final as death.

So let's put our trust in e. e. cummings's "deepest secret nobody knows," and promise to carry each other's heart. I'll carry your heart and you'll carry mine—full of memories of the good times we've had together. Then

---

death will be no more than the tinted glass window on the bus through which we have said hello and good-bye to each other so many times. Like that window it will be a little cold and a little hard. We won't be able to touch, but the warm feelings in our hearts will find their way to each other, I'm sure.

Acknowledgments

Without Al there would have been no Barbara.

Without Barbara there would have been no problem.

Without Karen and David there might have been no hope.

Without Bob Perske there would have been no book. He persuaded me to hang all my little outbursts onto an outline—until they came together.

Without teachers there would have been no lessons learned, and the teachers are almost too numerous to list: Gunnar and Rosemary Dybwad; Bank-Mikkelsen, Gesche Alberts, and Elna Skov; Bengt Nirje, Carl Grunewald, Wolf Wolfensberger, Helen Zauha, Linda Glenn, Shirley Dean, and Frank Menolascino; Hugh Lafave, Burton Blatt, Doug Biklen, and Dick Koch; Ed Pye, David Sokoloff, Charles Galloway, and Bill Bronston; Anne Shearer, Barbara Jessing, Mary Moore, Richard Lyon, Ed Sandtner, Naomi Gray, and Winifred Kempton; Dennis Pankratz, Al Zonca, and Ray Hudson.

A whole different cast of characters helped with the book itself. Betty Anglin, Hugh Lafave, the Dybwads, Ray Duff, Kris Hall, and Peter Jones read the first draft and red-penciled with abandon. Linda Warner volunteered the scholarly insights and critical abilities of her father, Wellman Warner, as an "outsider" to the field of mental retardation and a stranger to me. He has since become an insider and a friend! Robert Meyers gave me a big boost and critical advice when I needed it most.

Without Robert Petersen and his crew who let me use their erratic copying machine to duplicate my manuscript, I'd probably be in hock.

Barbara Mullen, John Gildersleeve, and Howard Martin freely offered technical assistance.

Linda Kusserow turned out to be an incredibly perceptive editor without whom I might still be chewing on my pencil.

I'm getting a little old and a little forgetful and have probably not mentioned any number of people who richly deserve it.

Thanks to you all.